Brian H...

Remr have the

POWER TO PERSEVERE !

POWER TO PERSEVERE

Inspiring Stories to Help You Get Through Challenging Moments

ALEXA NICOLE CUCCHIARA

NEW DEGREE PRESS

COPYRIGHT © 2019 ALEXA NICOLE CUCCHIARA

All rights reserved.

POWER TO PERSEVERE

Inspiring Stories to Help You Get Through Challenging Moments

ISBN   978-1-64137-302-9 *Paperback*

          978-1-64137-583-2 *Ebook*

I dedicate this book to...

My younger brother, Paul.

As the second oldest cousin of the bunch, I also dedicate this to Jessica, Alyssa, Deanna, Nicholas, Jonathan, Quinn, Bella, Olivia, Paulie, Big Al, Jake, Marco, and Christian. Use this book to help you persevere, loved ones.

Lastly, this book is for you. Yes, you. I dedicate this book to anyone who feels alone in whatever battle they are going through.

You got this!

Contents

You can either see yourself as
a wave in the ocean or you can
see yourself as the ocean.

—Oprah Winfrey

Acknowledgments

In creating this book, I had the opportunity to connect with unique humans—some that I personally knew and those that were strangers to me. I am humbled for every person God has led into my life to make this book the most perfect it can be. Thank you to everyone who spared their time, became vulnerable enough to share their story, and believed in my higher mission. Each conversation gave me the chance to dig deep and find a common thread that connected us all, something that I know will carry for a lifetime.

I never knew how much sacrifice and work went into writing a book: endless days and nights of researching, reaching out to experts in hope that they would hop on a 20 minute or hour interview over the phone, many, many, drafts on paper, lots of prayer, and patience. At the end, I realized that it takes more than just an idea, rather a tribe of believers. I am so humbled that I have been able to create something that will help others.

First and foremost, thank you to my family for believing in me. Mama, Papa, and Paul M., thank you for staying by my side throughout this journey.

Thank you Grandma Lillian for being my best friend and greatest cheerleader.

Thank you Dr. Owen O'Connor, Heya, Ashling, Laine, and my team of doctors and nurses for helping me be here today.

Thank you to my gal pals who have stayed by my side through thick and thin and to my faith-filled friends for keeping my spirits up.

Thank you to Haley Hoffman Smith for introducing me to Eric Koester.

Thank you to New Degree Press, especially, Eric Koester and Brian Bies, and my team of editors and designers for cheering me on through my toughest moments.

Lastly, thank you to everyone who gave me their time for a personal interview, pre-ordered the eBook, paperback, and multiple copies to make publishing possible, helped spread the word about *Power to Persevere* to gather amazing momentum, and help me publish a book I am proud of. I am sincerely grateful for all of your help.

Aidan Tracy	Juniper Shay
Alex Gallagher	Justine DeCristofaro
Alexander Palumbo	Katherine Sutton
Alyssa Lo Re	Katie Ionescu
Amanda Ianiri ~	Kieran O'Reilly
Amanda Innamorato	Krist Sokoli
Amanda Spiteri	Kristin and Nick Palumbo
Angela Bertorelli	Kristin Henn
Angela Ciuffo	Lana Stacy ~
Ann Marie Demaria	Larissa May ~
Anthony Finocchiaro	Laura Gallagher
Ashleigh Keogh *	Laura L R
Barbara Bruno *	Lauren Vecchio
Barbara Palumbo	Lexie Duval
Beth Mumm	Lia Koopman
Blanche Mackey	Lillian C. Morea
Bradley Kove	Lillian Cucchiara **~
Brian, Mercy, Elena, and Diana Turner *	Linda Casabene
Carlos Moreno	Lindsay Castro
Carly Beier	Lisa A. and Jim DeVilla
Carmine and Nancy Cirillo *	Lisa Skoglund
Carol Oster	Liz Isenring
Caroline Ricci	Madison Schott
Caroline Smoldt	Maria Broecker
Cheryl A. Crawford	Maria DiOrio

Christian Pankovcin	Mariateresa Libretti
Consuelo Castañuela Helbling	Marie DeFilippi
Deana Walker	Mark Bruno
Dennis J. Eickhorst	Mark Montalbano *
Devon McCaffrey	Mary Barbrack
Diane Grasso	Mary Carbonell Chapell
Dominica Dayton	Mary Ellen Miraglia
Donna Morea Coppola	Mary Lemmer
Ed Bosek *	Mary Vange
Elandas Miller	Matthew Kasabian
Elizabeth Paramonte	Matthew Kurzweil
Emily Love-Linay	Megan Mullaney
Emmanuel C. Durousseau	Megan O'Brien
Eric Koester	Michael Nicolia
Evelyn Hunter *	Michael Shokouhi ~
Evelyn Morris	Michaela Ceci *
Fran Colucci	Michelle Martone
Fran Miraglia	Nahi Ajaka
Frederick Dunau	Natasha Rockwell
George Lopez	Nicole Foster ~
Gina Palumbo	Patricia Contrabasso
Hal Rubin	Patricia Cuminale *
Ilir Bilali	Patricia O'Brien
Irene Stokes	Paul T, Gina, Paul M. Cucchiara *
Jack Ryan McNicholas	Peder Meller
Jack Witherspoon ~	Peggy and Sal Coppola
Jake Pfeffer	Peter Capotosto
James Merkel	Pina Santanna
Janina Diaz-Soto ~	Pina M. Chevalier
Jean Dunau	Rachel Craig
Jennice Chance	Regina Kernaghan
Jeraldo Vasquez	Renee Kinsella

Jesse Hunter	Rosemarie Bosek *
Jessica Bongiorno *	Roberta Miraglia
Jessica Colucci	Rosanna Russo
JJ Meador	Sam Santos-Shevett
Joan and Mike Cannon	Samuel Barandes
Joe Barrett	Sara Christoforides
Joe Colón	Sean Doherty
John Shea	Sharon Lopez *
John Walsh	Sofia Profita
John Willemsen *	Stephanie Palumbo ~
Johnmarco Coppola	Steve and Carmela Palumbo
Joseph A. Gullo	Terrence Duffy
Joseph Battista	Theresa Beier
Joseph Kopp *	Timos Pietris *
Joshua Hackett	Victoria A. Dengel *
Joy and Rex Duval ~	William Bernens *
Julia Morrison	William Cameron
Julia Pudimott	Yamilette M. Rich *
	Zachary Ashworth

*   Special Recognition - Multiple Copies/Campaign Contributions

**   Extra Special Recognition

~   Featured Interviewee

Introduction

I used to be scared like you. Then I told myself that we are all in the same position, so there must be more to life. Do not worry, Alexa.

—*PAUL T. CUCCHIARA*

"Is it out? Is it out?"

These were the first few words I remember saying as I finally came back into consciousness after my surgery. The nurses assured me the procedure went fine as they worked in tandem to move my body from the operating table to a wheelchair. I was overcome with relief, and my thoughts immediately turned to the tasks I had to fulfill before my first week of classes, which were beginning in just a few days.

On my way to the recovery room, I repeatedly reviewed my back-to-school checklist in my head: wash my clothes, pack my bedding, order my books, and buy appliances for my new college apartment. I started to panic. How was I going to do all of this with the excruciating and unbearable pain I was experiencing?

Within moments of arriving in recovery, all thoughts of school and checklists slipped away. My parents greeted me and, after stepping away for a moment, my dad handed me the phone. Groggy and fragile, I slowly grabbed the device and asked who it was. "Your surgeon, Dr. Godin," he replied.

"Hi, Alexa, the surgery went well. It is important that I let you know that there is an eighty percent chance you have Hodgkin's lymphoma, but..." my surgeon told me as I cut him off.

"Wait, do I have cancer?" I asked.

"It might be cancer, but it is curable," he replied.

I froze. Time froze. Everything around me stopped. He continued to speak on the line, but all I heard was silence. I felt like I blacked out, and maybe I did for a split second. I do not even remember seeing the reaction on my parents' faces. These were the *last* words I ever expected to hear after my biopsy. I was in disbelief.

"That is impossible! I am so healthy," I cried back.

"We have to wait one week for the pathology report to come back to one hundred percent confirm it," he replied.

A week later, on August 30, 2017, during the first week of what was supposed to be my junior year of college, I was hit with news no one wants to hear: "You have Hodgkin's lymphoma, a type of blood cancer that affects the lymphatic system," Dr. David Godin said.

The doctor left the room to grab some paperwork, and I immediately took out my phone to research the statistics. I found a report by MD Anderson Cancer Center that said this: "More than nine thousand people are diagnosed with Hodgkin's lymphoma in the United States each year...mainly in individuals between sixteen and thirty-four years of age." I was now one of them.

It was now the second time my family faced cancer. I had watched my grandfather, Melchiore, battle it for seven years. I knew what was coming. I felt trapped, like I was under the weight of a collapsed building. There was no way out. This was now my reality. Everything I was about to endure was out of my control, and I was terror-stricken.

After hearing this news, I had an inclination to call my grandmother for encouragement. I asked her to share with me uplifting stories about Grandpa Mel. I was desperate and needed reassurance that I was going to be okay. What she went on to reveal to me gave me the courage to see past the panic, pain, and fear. She gave me the determination to persevere.

Your grandfather was sick for months, but he refused to go to the doctor, which eventually caused him to be rushed to the hospital in an ambulance. After testing, we found out he had Stage 3 colon cancer, and the ammonia level in his blood caused him to go into a coma.

On the sixth day of his coma, while the family was visiting, his brother, Sal, a man of faith, came to the hospital with relics, holy water, oils, and rosary beads, and laid them around him. We then encircled your grandfather and started to pray very hard. While we were praying, Sal anointed him with the oils and water, and gently touched his body with the relics.

All of a sudden, your grandfather's body jerked and he opened his eyes. The whole family in the room started yelling for the doctors and nurses to come and see what just happened. Six days later, his awakening was unexpected. He was known as the miracle man.

A few months later, when he had recovered enough to com-municate, I asked Grandpa if he remembered seeing anything while he was in the coma, like God. He told me this: 'Before I got out of the coma, I was lying down somewhere. I looked around me, and there were hundreds of people also lying down next to me. All of a sudden, I felt God behind me. I didn't see him, but I felt him. He lifted up my hand, and he said to me, "It's not your time, you have to go back to help people." Next thing I knew, I turned around and came back.

Throughout the rest of his life, your grandfather took every opportunity he could to help others, whether he encouraged new patients he met in waiting rooms who expressed their fear of receiving chemotherapy, went on medical trials to test new drugs, or participated in other medical studies to help cure patients from burns and wounds, which ended up being successful. He kept his head high and attitude strong because of what God told him, and you can too.

She was right: I had the power within me to persevere. I immediately felt an almost electric buzz, and my fear was replaced with a deep, profound sense of gratitude. I was reassured there *was* more to life, and from that moment on, my grandfather became my inspiration to push through. If he used the gift of faith to accept the facts of the matter and overcome his anguish, I had the ability to follow his example and try to do the same.

It was very difficult at first, but I slowly built enough strength to take my life into my own hands. I was set on a path to reclaim my well-being through education. I watched videos, listened to podcasts, and read books on self-help and discovery, spirituality, the psyche of the mind, wellness, and nutrition. Eventually, I came to an important and invaluable realization after absorbing all this content: no matter our age, everyone experiences some type of adversity, be it big or small. No one is immune to this phenomenon. However, how we handle it is what sets us apart and inevitably defines us.

Within us, all of us, is the ability to shift the lens through which we interpret and experience our world. Regardless of individual circumstances, it is possible to strive for peace and serenity. We must come to terms with our circumstances and accept that the unexplainable and unfathomable battles we face are a constant test of our faith. In order to truly confront what we cannot control, we must also trust. Trust that the quality of the life we experience and our ongoing legacy is far more powerful than our pain. My grandfather paid forward this lesson.

We have to come to terms with ourselves and recognize that we can overcome our situation. And, whenever we are feeling lost, we need to remember that we have the ability to conquer the situation because we are our own rulers and control our response to what life throws at us, even for that which we have no plan or preparation. We control how we experience our stories and how they end. Rhonda Byrne, author of *The Magic*, the third book in one of the longest-running best-selling self-help book series of *The Secret*, essentially says the same thing:

Your life is in your hands. No matter where you are now, no matter what has happened in your life, you can begin to consciously choose your thoughts, and you can change your life. There is no such thing as a hopeless situation. Every single circumstance of your life can change!

My Gift of Inspiration
God gives us problems to push our resistance to sculpt our souls.

—TONY ROBBINS

This is a book of hope and inspiration. I want you to look at it like a toolbox. Use all the stories, quotes, and research in the coming chapters as fuel to help fill your soul and lift your spirits. They are here to help you recognize that you are not alone and have the power to persevere.

A little disclaimer if I may...Hey, I do not have all the answers. I do not think anybody does, but I have insight, even at this very young age. With what I was dealt, I gained a lot of clarity.

I often believed cancer was sure to be the end of me when it was my daily battle. As a survivor, I now know this was not the case. As great a gift as my survival are the hard-won lessons I have learned about my inner strength. For as long as I have the privilege of life, I will continue to face hardships. I now know that I can pull from within to overcome any hurdle. I think all the time: "If I could beat death, then nothing can stop me." My traumatic experience helped me learn how to become grounded, love my body like never before, find beauty in the world, and, most importantly, find purpose.

It took a lot of self-work and reflection to find myself where I am today on my life journey. There was no one to guide me. I had to figure it all out on my own. Although this was a challenging time, it was one that would forever shape my life and teach me lessons that I'll carry with me forever. Now it is my goal to spread the lessons I experienced to a wider audience. I want you to feel less alone and more empowered. I want you to proceed to live with optimism and grace so you can show up to the world as your best self.

Throughout this book, you will have the opportunity to use interactive reflection exercises as you gain insight from the following:

- My personal cancer experience
- Others who have also battled my illness, or have had limb loss, struggled with drug addiction, suffered from depression, and were homeless, to name a few
- Health professionals, life coaches, spiritual directors, and other certified professionals

Before reading any further, I want you to remember one thing: your life is worth living. Never have doubts about this one.

Sometimes, when we are at rock bottom, we may feel like there is no way out and have doubts about our self-worth. If we are open to changing our perspective, however, our worst nightmare has the potential to be our greatest gift. Our battle can help us develop the clarity to live fearlessly.

There is much more to life than we could ever imagine. We have to trust that our tragedies have meaning and purpose in our lives—that they are meant to mold us into the best version of ourselves. Remember Alexander Graham Bell's famous quote, "When one door closes, another opens; but we often look so long and so regretfully upon the closed door that we do not see the one which has opened for us."

As impossible as it might sound, try reframing your circumstances, even those that seem too much to bear. Rather than just lamenting your misfortune, attempt to acknowledge the wins, kindnesses from courageous souls around you, and hidden beauty of small moments.

We must keep our heads high, stay positive, move forward, and roll with the punches. With that, trust the battle. Trust the struggle. Trust yourself. Trust *it*, and know you can create your own strength. You have the power to persevere.

Are you ready to embark on a new journey and become the best version of yourself?

Let's do it.

Chapter 1

Awakening

Once the soul awakens, the search begins and you can never go back. From then on, you are inflamed with a special longing that will never again let you linger in the lowlands of complacency and partial fulfillment. The eternal makes you urgent. You are loath to let compromise or the threat of danger hold you back from striving toward the summit of fulfillment.

—*JOHN O'DONOHUE, ANAM CARA: A*
BOOK OF CELTIC WISDOM

I want to begin this book by sharing with you how I got to where I am today—how I came out on the other side and started to persevere. I was awakened, and I have a feeling you are too.

If you are reading this right now, you are probably looking for hope. Perhaps you are in physical pain, or maybe you are emotionally distraught. You might be searching for a way out of your discomfort, or for a glimmer of light and hope. Maybe you feel discouraged and are afraid to try a new experience and need guidance, or perhaps you know someone else who is in desperate need of a reset and are using this book to help them. Before I found peace in what was weighing me down, I went through these same trials.

Remember, no one is alone. Spiritual philosopher Amit Ray says "You are eternally connected with everyone." So, if we are connected, then we are all one and can learn from each other with confidence and ease.

Story Time

It all happened the first week of my junior year of college in 2018. My second one. The official one. The one where I did not have to drop out of school for the whole school year, in 2017.

I transferred to a new institution closer to home, and although I was excited to start this new chapter, I felt very out of place. It was my first time back in school in over a year. Because I was out of this environment for so long, jumping into a fast-paced, day-to-day school routine seemed daunting to me. I was so used to being isolated and going to see doctors every day that I had forgotten what it felt like to study and socialize with my peers.

Not only was I in a different headspace but my appearance was also different. My short, curly hair reminded me of Nick Jonas during the peak of his teenage career. And, on top of that, I had some noticeable scars on my body. Honestly, I felt like I did not even know who I was anymore. Although I was dejected, I was propelled into a magnificent awakening, and suddenly, I became aware of the larger picture in life.

One Tuesday afternoon in class, a thought came to me after I opened my notepad, secured my pen tighter between my thumb and index finger, and placed the tip onto my college-ruled, single subject notebook. As I was trying to write the date, I felt my muscles tightening, aching, and throbbing. I wanted to fall out of my chair, onto the ground, and curl up in a ball. I wanted someone to carry me to my bed, tuck me into my sheets, and let me lie there, alone. I was anxious because I wanted to feel normal again, but I was still feeling the effects of chemotherapy in my body. I was fatigued and weak. It felt like I got hit by a train.

During this time, I recalled a quote from a video by Joel Osteen called "Overcoming Weariness" that I heard after my first chemotherapy infusion. It stated, "If you will stay in faith, God will not only renew your strength, he'll renew your health." I reminded myself to keep having faith because it was all part of the healing process. I said to myself, "If I was able to get through chemotherapy, I can get through anything. Have faith, Alexa. Trust the process."

My professor distracted me. "Alexa?" she called.

I jerked my head up and replied, "Here" with the most fabricated smile as everyone turned to me. Great. The spotlight was on me, and this was the last thing I wanted. But then I noticed something. After my name was called for attendance, I realized the student next to me was glowing. And, surprisingly, it was from me!

The subtle light creeping through the blinds was directly hitting my metallic gold pullover hoodie, making everything around me brighter. Just like that—the dim light within me was shining even through my misery. Before my very own eyes, I started to see the truth in Osteen's message: have faith.

When class ended, I slowly bent down and grabbed my gray backpack off the floor and walked down the stairs and through the building's side doors. The second

I took a step into the fresh air, I was overwhelmed by the calmness of the outdoors. I felt the sun rays and subtle humidity kiss the surface of my skin; I took a deep breath, shut my eyes, tilted my head back, and expressed gratitude. It was happening. Faith was creeping its way in. My attitude changed, and I was able to turn my agony around with just the simple gift of Mother Nature. It was miraculous. And, the funny part—it happened at school. This was the last place I thought I was going to experience any healing. What were the odds?

Afterward, I wondered if any of the students running to their next class felt the same as I did. Did they ever feel pain as strong as mine? Did they ever go through traumatic experiences where they felt no hope? I went back to my room, unpacked my bag from the day, sat down at my desk, and unlocked my phone.

I opened Instagram to respond to a message I had received, but something on my homepage grabbed my attention. It was a bright green icon from Luna Peak Company—a community website that creates books and products to inspire and celebrate life. I clicked through the stories on the upper banner of the app. Once open, a photo appeared with text written across it. I read it and my jaw dropped.

Luna Peak was making one last stop to New York City for a final round of photographing 100 survivors of all types of cancer and interviewing each one on the wisdom gained throughout their personal journey. I realized I was no longer alone: there were more people than I could have imagined who actually had similar issues. It was not just me and Grandpa Melchiore.

Without a second thought, I immediately applied. I was not even a year into remission, but I remembered how overwhelmed I felt when I was given my diagnosis and knew I had to help others with my voice.

Fast forward a few weeks later, to the morning of the photo shoot. I got cold feet. I was scared and hesitant. I started thinking about all the negative things that could come with publicly opening up about my cancer experience, such as judgment and shame. I did not want to be labeled as "the sick one" or have anyone think lesser of me because of my uncommon experience. I called my friend Nicole, who was also part of Luna Peak Company's initiative. I expressed my concerns and asked her what to do. She encouraged me, telling me I had so much to share and could influence and help the lives of many. She was right.

Why was I second-guessing myself? Why was I questioning the purpose of my battle? In my heart, I knew I was sent on this journey for a reason. This cancer experience was supposed to prepare me for the next phase in my life and fulfill a deep desire to help others. I needed to have faith in myself. I threw on a pair of jeans, slipped into a shirt, grabbed my denim jacket, tied the laces on my sneakers, and hopped into an Uber. And off I went to the photo studio.

When I arrived, Melody Lomboy-Lowe and her niece Gracelyn Bateman, the creators behind this project, asked me a series of questions for their book:

- If you could tell yourself on the day of diagnosis something now, what would it be?
- What advice would you give to someone that has been recently diagnosed?
- Did you have any rituals or things that helped you cope?
- Did you have a support team, and what did they do for you?

When I was answering these questions, I felt like I had so much insight to share. This was the first time I started to see the meaning behind what I had been through. My life was finally serving a purpose.

A few hours after I left the photo shoot and had my interview, I ran into one of my old elementary school friends, Jake.

"Alexa, you have this energy about you right now. You are glowing. Where are you coming from?" he asked.

I smiled and humbly responded with excitement, "I just had a photoshoot for a cancer survivor project!"

"That's amazing, Lex!" he exclaimed.

Jake became my source of confirmation. He made me realize that I needed to keep spreading my voice, light, and wisdom. I knew I had planted a seed to help my community, and this was just the beginning. I returned to a few memories I had from when I was going through treatment. I recalled how my friends and I would joke around about how I should write a book one day. I thought, "If I was able to inspire and impact my friends, and now Luna Peak's audience, why not actually write that book?"

At that moment, I began to remember the wisdom I had gained from all the literature I had read, videos I had watched, and podcasts I had listened to while going through treatment. I could not let my knowledge go to waste. Whether it was from inspiration I collected from the Bible, Tao Te Ching, and other books; videos of TEDx talks; sermons by pastors like TD Jakes and Steven Furtick; spiritual teachers on YouTube like Leeor Alexandra and Aaron Doughty, I realized that people could benefit from all that I learned, from my unique perspective.

I finally had my awakening—my "aha" moment. That night, I started on a mission. I took out a piece of paper and outlined what I wanted to communicate to the world. I made it a goal to talk to people of all ages about their trials and tribulations, and create a community of my own. *This* is how I was going to help people. Channeling my grandfather, his faith and my own, I knew my journey forward was going to serve a higher purpose.

Action Plan and Lesson

The reason for your agony might bear meaning, just like mine did for me. Perhaps you are experiencing this distress for a reason. The universe might be trying to tell you, "Hey, you need to understand how this feels in order to help someone else going through a similar experience." And, with that, you can use your anguish to not only help others persevere but also yourself.

This can be your opportunity to catapult yourself into a new direction. This can be the start of a new chapter. Let's look at Melody, for example. Her experience with pediatric cancer influenced her to start an initiative to help other cancer patients through Luna Peak Company, LLC. Today, she has touched the lives of thousands.

Even if your adversity is chronic and enduring, you can be a sign of hope, faith, and purpose for someone else. It is quite brave, if you think of it. I would suggest engaging in simple activities like volunteering at hospitals, donating to shelters, serving food at soup kitchens, starting a nonprofit, or organizing fundraisers. Hey, maybe you can even write a book like me.

There are so many ways you can shine your magic onto others and be that light of hope. All you need to do is recognize the opportunity, and the rest will come. Imagine how you can and will make others feel!

Leave your legacy.

Reflect
How will you turn your battle into your purpose?

Chapter 2

Acceptance

Life is a series of natural and spontaneous changes. Don't resist them—that only creates sorrow. Let reality be reality. Let things flow naturally forward in whatever way they like.

—LAO TZU

Becoming awakened, as I discussed in my last chapter, was not exactly the first step I used to heal myself. If you think about it, it was actually acceptance. Remember how I second-guessed myself about not wanting to open up about my cancer journey but then decided to stop listening to these fears and share my light? I could have stayed in denial, but I surrendered. I told myself that cancer was always going to be part of my life, but it did not have to be my whole story. It was just an experience I could use to help others.

Seeing the outcome of my acceptance is what ultimately awakened me. I believe it all started with my perspective and state of mind. You have to come to terms with what you're facing and take on a more casual attitude: it is what it is. Understandably, you'll be angry at first, but staying angry will not benefit you in any way. Whatever you are going through might be tough, but if you have already done everything you could to change it, then you need to move on and tell yourself, "This is where I am today, but every day I am growing and persevering. I will be okay."

Acceptance was difficult for me when all I could think about was all of the memories I was missing out on at school with my friends, meals I could not eat because of my nausea, and hair I could not brush because it had all fallen out. This was certainly not the year I planned. Whenever my mother caught me going down a dark path, she said, "Alexa, if you are doing the best you can, then that is good enough. Sometimes we cannot control certain situations. Take each day as it comes, and with the grace of God, you will get through this. Stop comparing yourself to who you were before and looking at what you are missing out on. Every day is part of the healing process. It will only get better."

She was right. What purpose was becoming upset about the life I wish I had serving me? This is when I started to become mindful of what was triggering my mood.

It took a lot of courage and strength to acknowledge and welcome these negative thoughts. After doing this, I would repeat to myself, "I accept my life. I accept my body. I accept where I am today." This allowed me to release my anger, which, ultimately, helped me heal.

Life coach Allison Carmen says that acceptance is making peace with something in our lives that either causes physical or emotional pain. It is the beginning to or of a new way of overcoming our problems. She said,

Acceptance is about not arguing with reality and letting go of the pain that we experience when we resist what is happening.

The minute you recognize something is totally out of your control, that is your signal to let go and try to make the best of what is happening.

When you don't accept something, it is a pain that can never go away, and when you do accept something that you don't like, it's a pain that can evolve. You can stop caring about the issue, it can start to mean less, you can learn to live with the situation, or it just changes over time. Acceptance also allows our emotions to glide someplace else when we are ready

We realize this is just an experience we are having and every-thing in life changes. This is when we become very thankful for the uncertain future. If we don't know what will happen next, this means that things can get better, or we could find a way to live with whatever we're experiencing and still be okay.

Story Time

Two-time cancer survivor Bianca Muñiz was also able to live in peace through acceptance. When Bianca was eleven years old and in sixth grade, she was sent to the doctors to receive X-rays on her knees due to a condition known as Osgood-Schlatter disease, which created painful bumps on her bones because they were growing too fast.

A few months later, she couldn't stand up and called her mom for help. She was rushed to the doctor, and when she was lying down on the examination table, the doctors discovered something alarming. It was a bump in her pelvic area. Bianca was then rushed to the hospital, and three days later she had to undergo surgery to take out her right ovary.

"It all happened very fast," she said.

The surgeons then discovered that Bianca had an aggressive type of cancer that caused the growth of tumors on organs. She immediately went through six months of chemotherapy at the Maria Fareri Children's Hospital, and after, she had laparoscopic surgery to remove the rest of the tumors the doctors could not get to during the beginning of her diagnosis. Although Bianca's circumstances were rough, she always stuck with her own motto:

"If I am alive, I am fine."

Bianca went through treatment throughout seventh grade and made the most out of her life during this time. She accepted her circumstances and did not let them control her:

I got a lead as Gabriella in the musical High School Musical at school. I did not want to drop out of it, so I begged my parents and doctors to make a deal with me. I had to get my blood count tested regularly, and if it was too low, I would have to wear a face mask, but if it wasn't, then I could go to rehearsal. This is what got me through this [time in the hospital]. I would practice my lines and sing in the hospital every week so I could go to rehearsal and perform.

After seventh grade ended, Bianca stopped treatment. When she entered eighth grade, she, unfortunately, had a difficult time adjusting back to her normal life. She explained that not only did she have a new hairstyle, but she was insecure because she gained weight from treatment. This caused her to develop bulimia.

My mother found out [about my eating disorder] right away, and then reassured me that my body was affected. I needed to give it time to recover, and that my weight would go away without me having to do anything. I immediately stopped [my binge-purge cycle], and my body slowly went back to normal.

It was a difficult time and transition, but obviously, my mother was right. I had to accept her words and believe in them. Once I did, I started to slowly see changes in my body.

[After having cancer in seventh grade], I became aware of my body. I always checked my body and felt around to make sure everything was okay. I noticed that I kept getting little tumors in my breasts; they were all benign and the doctors did not want to turn me into a cutting board again, so we left them. A few months before graduating college at twenty-one, I discovered a new lump that was significantly different from the other ones. I went back to the doctors, and once again they said because they didn't want to turn me into a cutting board, we would keep an eye on it and see if it changed. A year later, after graduating college, switching insurance, and finding a new team of doctors, when I finally went back [to

the doctors], it had grown significantly. There were multiple tumors at that point. The radiologist was extremely concerned and scheduled me to get biopsies two days later.

I got a call from my doctors at work, and they told me I had stage 2 triple positive (TP) breast cancer. I was pretty relaxed and said, 'Cool, would you mind calling my mom and telling her? I don't want to be the one.' I then went in for genetic testing and found out I had a mutation called TP53, also known as Li-Fraumeni Syndrome. I had a double mastectomy, three and a half months of chemotherapy, and a year of other cancer treatments like Herceptin and PERJETA.

This time having cancer, I was like, 'This is happening. This is who I am. This is my life. We will just deal with it. We will do it.'

There was never a moment where I didn't think I would be fine. I took [this second cancer diagnosis] as a sign from the universe. This happened to me already once, so maybe I can use [breast cancer] for a higher good and to help, I started to blog and post on Instagram for other people my age going through what I was going through.

Today, I just try to do things that I know are good for my body and remind myself that feelings do not last. I tell myself that everything is temporary, that I am okay and just going through a difficult emotional time right now.

Whatever your obstacle or situation is, you have the power to change it, but if you cannot change it, you can't control it, so then just accept it. There is no point in fear or worry. Just trust whatever the situation you are in is meant to be and make the best of it.

Do not let yourself stay stuck in whatever negative feelings you are having. If I did that, I would not be on tour singing, performing at Madison Square Garden, and enjoying life right now.

Action Plan and Lesson

It is important to let life flow at its own natural pace. You will begin to see how things will unleash and unravel before your eyes, just like Bianca did. She did not let her cancer get in the way of her highest value: singing. She accepted her circumstances and continued to pursue her dreams without worrying about what was out of her control. She was ultimately able to persevere.

Don't believe so? That is fine; I can relate. But I would like to remind you that if you refrain from acceptance, then you become disconnected from reality and succumb to pessimism. This attitude will only exacerbate any stress and lead to more problems.

Think of it like this. When you are driving in traffic, you can't control that it might make you late for your corporate dinner event. Thus, you just have to accept that there is congestion and there is nothing you can do about it. You could go into road rage, but that would just raise your blood pressure and possibly put you and everyone around you in danger. Instead, you should be patient and see what plays out. Maybe the traffic is saving you from a car crash you could have gotten into.

Whenever you are upset, remember that you have the ultimate gift: life. If you are alive, then you are fine, as Bianca would say.

Because the affirmation "If I am alive, I am fine" worked for Bianca, I will help you come up with your own motto that will get you through your individual battle and cope. When I was undergoing treatment, I also created my own affirmations, which I will talk more about later in the book, to help me accept all that I was going through.

Here are a few I repeated to myself every morning:

- I am whole, loved, and complete.
- I am blessed by God and the universe every day.
- I am safe and secure.

- I am a warrior and I will beat this fight.

If you are having trouble thinking of some, start small. Write three simple phrases down and try to repeat them for one week while you are in the shower, brushing your teeth, or getting ready for bed. Repeat them in your head, sing them out loud, or write them down. Afterward, tap into your feelings. If you repeat them over time, you will start to truly believe them. I am confident that you will feel a little more liberated and free.

Evidently, it is up to *us* to make the decision to accept the reality of our situation. At the end of the day, why should we stress over something we cannot control? Let go and let God take control, as my grandmother would tell me. Let go and let the universe take control, as my friend Alyssa says.

Reflect
What is holding you back from acceptance?

What mantras will you say every day to help change your mindset?

Chapter 3

Changing Perspective

When you change the way you look at things, the things you look at change.

—DR. WAYNE DYER

Changing the way you look at the obstacles and challenges you are faced with can play a key role in the way you live your everyday life. It will allow you to turn dark into light and sorrow into peace. It first comes down to perspective which is the attitude you adopt for a given circumstance.

Anytime something that was not in my favor occurred during chemotherapy, I would try to reframe the meaning of it. For instance, one time my nurses tried to administer one of my treatments, but could not seem to manage it. They accessed my PowerPort, a device that was surgically placed into my chest to allow me to receive chemotherapy, numerous times. I had eight different shots of saline injected into the device over the course of an hour and different blood thinners to help dissolve what they diagnosed as a clot, causing extreme nausea that almost made me sick. We were frustrated because I had already taken my cocktail of medications and steroids for my pre-chemo prep protocol.

We eventually had to give up. I was sent home and instructed to travel an hour to another oncology center the next day to get a specific blood thinner to reverse the clot. The whole process was chaotic and caused havoc. The journey seemed never-ending, and I was losing hope. "Was I going to be cursed with having another clot?" I thought the night before our next attempt.

As I caught myself going down a negative path, I quickly reframed my perspective and thought that perhaps this was a blessing in disguise. Maybe if I had received the treatment the day prior, a worse complication could have occurred.

What ended up happening was that I was able to secure another peaceful evening with my family without the aftereffects of chemotherapy ruining my night. We made my favorite homemade meal, tagliatelle con ragù alla Bolognese, and watched a movie. Afterward, I learned that I needed to start becoming more patient and trusting. If not for this event, I would not have had an extra night free from even worse nausea and pain from the treatment—this night was my gift of freedom.

In general, my entire journey from diagnosis to remission is an example I used to help me persevere in the year to come. I told myself that if I needed to drop out of school for one whole year to become healthy again, I needed to use this time to pursue my passions, discover my true self, and transform my life. Even though I felt depleted and defeated many mornings, I kept my hopes high and reminded myself of the intentions I had set.

I can now say that I appreciate the time I had to myself. I spent it wisely and purposefully, reflecting on myself and what I wanted for the rest of my life when this battle was over. I now feel more humbled, whole, and complete. Cancer became my opportunity to evolve, mature, and grow because of the way I perceived it.

Story Time
Larissa May is another young female who also saw her defeat as an opportunity for change. Her journey started during her sophomore year at prep school, when she started recognizing the reality of her mental health

challenges. These brought her an overwhelming wave of emotions that she could not control.

During this year at school, it was really the first time that I recognized I was dealing with mental health issues. But at that point in my life, I didn't really know what mental health was. I do not ever remember it being a topic in my household, or it being something we talked about in school; [mental health] was just referred to as stress.

I had a lot on my plate, I was a perfectionist, and I really wanted to get into a top college, Vanderbilt, so I quit all of my creative endeavors to achieve this goal, which I ended up accomplishing, even though I devoted my entire life to [creativity] before. During this time, I was having panic attacks to the point where I had to lie flat in my bed. There were times that I actually thought that I was having a heart attack, but it was really because of having a panic attack. I was also very suicidal at the time.

There was a specific night when I really wanted to die at a Sweet Sixteen birthday party. I was so miserable. I was in so much pain, emotionally, to the point where I stopped caring about what I looked like. I would sometimes lay in bed for ten minutes just to be able to pull myself back up, function, and get back to studying. A lot of it was just created by personal pressure, and I think that is reflective of what pressure does to someone and what pressure in society does to individuals.

During my time in college, I moved to Los Angeles to intern for a brand internship with Sincerely Jules, a fashion blogger and business owner, and a celebrity PR company. During that time, I'd started a fashion blog and started to use social media as a way to connect with other creatives in LA because I didn't know anyone, and to top it off, I navigated the city on a bike with a broken chain.

I came back to Vanderbilt after the summer was over and spiraled back into a depressive episode, and my best friend at the time, who was my new roommate, moved out of my room because of my depression. I was really, really alone. I had to face some hard realities.

[In my dorm room], it was just me and an empty bed, and my friends dropped off the face of the earth because I was not going out anymore; I had no one. I could not get up to go to class for two weeks. I should have taken the semester off, but my family encouraged me to push through.

It was really, really challenging. I was going to the psychological center every day. But during that time, I was still going out to take photos for my Instagram and my fashion blog because I wanted to make it seem, you know, like I was okay. I tried to get into my old laptops and other technology because I really wanted to see things that I'd written, or videos that I created before.

Fast forward another couple years: I luckily made it through that depressive episode and really started to find my way through the creative community in Nashville, meeting and collaborating with a lot of my friends who are now very successful bloggers, videographers, and photographers.

During my senior year, I had panic attacks and nervous breakdowns, specifically during one of my jobs. I was running from Betsey Johnson's last show by Penn Station, downtown to cover Diane von Furstenberg's publication at AOL, front row. I was not taking care of myself, and I started freaking out.

I completely face-planted and fell on the floor, cut open my knee, broke my phone, and said to myself, 'Enough is enough. This is ridiculous. I am having a mental breakdown, and no one is seeing the truth on social media, only these beautiful photos of me published in Elle. If this is how I am going to live my life, it is not going to be okay. Everything about this is wrong.'

Just as the stress of the fashion world consumed Larissa in a negative way, she started to change the way she looked at the incident. She knew that this part of her life was meant to lead her somewhere else. Larissa started a movement.

This dream [of being part of the fashion world] that I loved was so miserable to me, and at that point, I needed to do something differently. So after [the shows in New York City], I came home and decided I wanted to shift my head a little bit and start a movement on Instagram.

My dream was fashion, it was like through [these specific fashion shows] that I realized that was not my dream. My dream was really to change the world.

I realized that part of why I was going through this was because there was something bigger for me. I think that as soon as I realized that, I was able to push through it. That sort of change helped me get through it, even though it was incredibly painful.

When Larissa went back to Nashville, where Vanderbilt University is located, she drew a logo with the words "Half the Story" on a sticker in her college dorm room. Little did she know, this idea would turn into an accepted grant from her art school and into an official nonprofit. organization.

The basis of #HalfTheStory was to embrace the other "half" of the story that was displayed on social media. Larissa wanted to expose the struggle behind people's lives. Although it might seem like someone is having a great time, you do not know what they are experiencing or how they got there, similarly to Larissa, for example. She looked like she was having the time of her life, but she was not. Her experience was not glamorous but rather disastrous, and she was distraught and broken (literally).

Larissa officially launched the platform her senior year. During the beginning of this new passion project, she started speaking to small groups on campus, who then shared their stories.

"One girl even used #HalfTheStory as a way to come out about her own sexuality," Larissa explained. "And then people from all around the world started to submit their stories onto the platform."

Larissa started to get a lot of press and was featured on Good Morning America and in *Time* magazine, among other publications. This is when #HalfTheStory took off.

[Posting on social media] can be a really powerful tool if done the right way. We started having these conversations about

social media and mental health before they actually started. Today, we are a 501(c)(3) nonprofit.

Our goal is to be an educational platform to first, change the conversation around social media and mental health; second, build out a media platform with educational videos and information about mental health; and third, create a larger foundation so we can subsidize mental health resources around the world.

Today, @halfthestory has over twenty-five thousand followers and has been represented in over eighty countries. They are continuing their mission to allow others to look at both sides of someone's story to ignite perspective and compassion. Instead of using social media as a way to celebrate success, the platform has been inspiring others to reveal their realities.

Throughout her time running this platform, Larissa has come up with some advice for anyone dealing with any struggle. She suggested that if you are going through something mentally, sit with your feelings, see where you are at, and then try to find a friend you can trust to confide in. Even if we are still in emotional pain, we can use our faith to push us through. Larissa explained that the only way to approach the unknown is to have a faith rocket.

"Believe in yourself and do it. So, just have faith. I launch my rockets and hope they land somewhere among the stars," she said.

Action Plan and Lesson

Larissa found purpose in her most vulnerable moments and turned it into a movement. This ultimately helped both herself and others persevere. This is why It is crucial for you to do the same. You need to learn how to change your perspective and positively frame your narrative.

There have been multiple studies that support the notion of creating a positive framework. Psychosom Med discovered that patients with acute coronary syndrome (ACS) had significant recovery in just twelve months when they displayed a positive outlook versus those who did not. This attitude influenced them to stop smoking, eat more fresh foods, and become more physically active. Their psychological well-being was less depressed, and they were able to adapt to circumstances better.

Another theory, from Dr. Joe Dispenza, a neuroscientist and author of *You Are the Placebo*, states that the way that we can change our thoughts, we alter the way our genes function, which changes our overall well-being and health. The way to do this is by changing your perception through mentally rehearsing what you want your new experience to be.

By keeping your focus on [the future] and not letting any other thoughts distract you, in a matter of moments, you turn down the volume on the neural circuits connected to the old self, which begins to turn off the old genes, and you fire and wire new neural circuits, which initiated the right signals to activate new genes in new ways...[and] at this point, your brain and body are no longer a record of the past; they are a map to the future—a future that you created in your mind. Your thoughts become your experience, and you just become the placebo.

Dr. Dispenza mentioned that the credibility behind his theory has been one that has been believed for decades. He justified this by referring to the research gathered by multiple studies:

- Mayo Clinic, which lasted over the course of thirty years
- Medical School of Georgia, which lasted twenty-five years
- Yale, which lasted twenty-three years

All resulted in the same conclusion: those who had a better attitude and were optimistic had a longer life span and were physically and mentally healthier.

The National Science Foundation also published an article revealing that the average person has between twelve thousand and sixty thousand thoughts per day. Eighty percent are negative, and 95 percent are repeated from the previous day. So, imagine how much self-sabotage you could cause yourself if you constantly perceived every adverse moment you are faced with through a negative lens. Changing your outlook will help you fall far from this statistic.

Let's say you planned a dinner date with the person you have had your eye on for months. Things are not going as you prepared for during your night out. You have nothing in common and cannot hold a conversation. As you excuse yourself from the table to use the restroom, your menu falls on the floor. You graciously bend down to pick it up, but then you hear a tear. The back of your jeans suddenly split in half, exposing your rear end. You have two options here.

Option 1: You can become embarrassed and let your frustration ruin the rest of your night.

Option 2: You can take the accident as an opportunity to look at this wardrobe malfunction as a blessing in disguise and have faith that this was the universe's way of giving you the opportunity to remove yourself from one of the most awkward social engagements you have yet to have. Not only this, but you can now buy yourself those jeans you have been wanting to get so you can stand in confidence during your next date. Boo-yah!

That was a trivial example, but you get the point. If you reframe the outcome to each aggravating situation, you are giving yourself the opportunity to rewire the way you habitually think. Yes, it takes time and practice, but I assure you, it works.

The way I would start practicing this is by making a pros and cons list. Grab a piece of paper and divide the sheet into two columns. On the left, write the pros, and the right, the cons. This will help you visually see the best- and worst-case scenarios and that the latter may be a list of silly excuses or simply unlikely possibilities.

Reflect
What is something in your life that could use a different perspective, and how will you change it?

Chapter 4

Fight Your Fears

Fear keeps us focused on the past or worried about the future. If we can acknowledge our fear, we can realize that right now we are okay. Right now, today, we are still alive, and our bodies are working marvelously. Our eyes can still see the beautiful sky. Our ears can still hear the voices of our loved ones.

—THICH NHAT HANH

I have a secret for you...

I refused to tell anybody about my illness when I was first diagnosed and did not want anybody to know I was sick. I was not sure how people would react. I battled opening up to friends and family about my reality at the time of my diagnosis. I did not want anyone to know that I had cancer because I did not know anyone my age who did. I felt I was faced with an abnormal circumstance and was ashamed to admit to it.

According to research done by The Abramson Cancer Center of the University of Pennsylvania, out of over 88 million, only seventy thousand young adults in the United States from the ages of fifteen to thirty-nine are diagnosed with cancer each year. That is less than 1 percent of the population.

With that information, you can imagine how alone I felt. And, because of this isolation, I did not want others to view me any differently because I knew I was not different at my core. I constantly worried about being judged. I also did not want to bring this heavy topic to a social environment. I was afraid it would make others feel uncomfortable.

Although I had this fear bottled up inside me, I slowly broke out of my shell each day. It first started when I told my grandmother and brother that I had cancer. Then, I immediately shared the same information with other close family members and college roommates, explaining to them that I could no longer live with them. I slowly started to break the news to concerned family members, who were adamantly encouraging me to update them on what my doctors were saying, and then to my classmates, who were texting me why I was not in class. I finally became comfortable enough to talk to random strangers on the street, in restaurants, and in stores about my diagnosis.

With all that I was going through, I started to accept the fact that I fit into that small statistic given by Abramson Cancer Center. It was my new reality, and that was okay. Although it was getting easier to open up about all that I was going through, I still faced moments of doubt.

Story Time

One day as I was about to leave my apartment to travel up to my oncologist's office for an appointment, my phone beeped. I read the message, placed my phone down on my bed, and stared at it for a moment, hesitating to answer.

It was a text message from my friend Mike. He was in Manhattan for an interview and wanted to see me. Of course I wanted to meet my friend, but there was also a part of me that felt too ashamed for him to see me in my condition. I was bald, and the pigment in my skin was practically gray. I took a moment to reflect on his concern about my general well-being and figured it was best for us to meet in person. I picked up my phone and texted him back.

We met in front of the Stephen A. Schwarzman Building, the main branch of the New York Public Library located in Midtown. I was welcomed by his warm hug as he said, "Alexa, you are the reason why I am getting through this semester. I look at everything you have been going through and have been looking at life differently." I looked at Mike, smiled, and got teary-eyed. I was overwhelmed with a sense of happiness like I had never experienced before.

It took me a while to let this sink in. I did not feel like I was doing anything; I was simply standing in front of Mike, hiding my bald head under my black Nike cap and bundled up in my blanket scarf, which was tucked into my warm, black-leather biker jacket. I guess you could say I looked like a strong and fierce woman that could hop on her motorcycle and speed down the highway.

After his greeting, I asked Mike how his interview with NBC went. Mike told me that he was conflicted with what to do with his career. He was on a pre-med track at school but had a passion for writing. His interview did not go as well as planned. He was discouraged and was thinking about giving up because he had no experience either in class or through a job.

He did not know how to take a leap onto a new path. He was afraid to leave behind all of his hard work studying science. He was conflicted by these thoughts. At that moment, I realized something else: life is too short.

I told him, "You need to follow your heart. Look at me. Anything can happen to you at any given time, so you need to make sure you are happy. You can do it." He looked at my cap as if he was trying to visualize what I looked like underneath it, smiled, and responded, "You are right." I gave him the courage that assured him that he should not be afraid.

Months later, he called me and told me that he had listened to what I said and had started writing during his free time and had landed his first writing job. He was happier than ever before and was glad that he had listened to my advice. At first, he was too timid to take a leap onto an unknown path, but he was able to do something he thought was too difficult to achieve. Hearing this encouraged me to take pride in my appearance and fearlessly walk the streets of Manhattan with confidence.

Action Plan and Lesson

Whenever we go through dire situations, whether it is something as simple as Mike's story or as life-threatening as a cancer diagnosis, we immediately produce the emotions of fear and anxiety.

Dr. Michael Brustein, a New York City clinical psychologist, specifically works with patients to overcome these feelings. According to his research, the reason these emotions occur is because after we feel lost or lose a sense of control, we become afraid to face a similar or worse experience. Although this type of tension and apprehension has a negative effect, we can actually use this as a tool to uplift us. He said:

We usually tend to see the world crumble as it feels no longer safe because our whole model of life view changes. The result could be very isolating as one tries to navigate who they are, and with this, there can be a withdrawing and a pointless kind of perspective emerging.

Then, as growth starts to combine your old world with your new world, you have a richer understanding as to, yes, it is not completely safe, but it is also not a horrible place. There is a nuanced, synthesized perspective.

With any fear you have, the only way to manage it is to face it. The pay-off and reward for confronting it will be much richer. Yes, there can be discomfort or shame, but facing it is the reward. What you get is much more powerful. It might feel safe to avoid it, but it is a cost-benefit.

It is clear that when you face your fear, a weight will be lifted off your shoulders and you will feel like you can persevere through anything. This was the case for Mike, and this was the case for me. He was able to pursue his dreams, and I was able to continue to live in courage without the fear of judgment.

Pastor T.D. Jakes says that it is fear that holds people back. It will not lead to a positive end because it is not coming from faith. Mike believed in his core that he wanted to pursue a career in writing, and he did. I knew I needed to stop caring about what people thought of me, which I did. Both of us now continue to persevere without any hesitations.

To face your fears I suggest you step out of your comfort zone:

- Afraid of opening up about your experience? Take baby steps and confide in someone you trust.

- Afraid of feeling alone? Find online support groups and make friends who know what you are going through.
- Afraid of never finding hope? Do research on ways others managed their pain and use their tips to help fuel you!

Reflect

How will you live fearlessly?

Chapter 5

Follow Your Fire

Be fearless in the pursuit of what sets your soul on fire.

—JENNIFER LEE

There is something quite magical about pursuing what makes you spark and feel whole. In the last chapter, you were able to see how Mike mustered the courage to find his spark as a result of the inspiration I found in bravely standing up to my fears. From our experiences, I realized that when we feel trapped, something in life can catapult us in a new direction and give us the nudge to embark on something we might have been hesitant to pursue before.

When you focus your energy on something that produces an abundance of joy, there is an overwhelming feeling that starts to ignite in your heart. You are more energized and feel powerful. This is when you start to persevere because doing what you love helps bring more vitality into your life.

While experiencing troubling times during and after treatment, engaging in activities that gave me pleasure helped me get through each day. Whether I occupied myself in creative work like painting, visited museums and local art galleries, or sewed clothes, I felt at home with who I was and thrived.

In fact, there was this one day that I decided to raid my closet from my denim collection and recycle my unworn pieces into something new. I ended up spending the whole day meticulously cutting the outer layers of the inseam of each leg, layering, pinning, and stitching them into belts. My imagination not only allowed me to turn the old into new, but because I was in flow with what I enjoyed, I did not focus on my nausea and completely lost track of time. The day flew by and I was one day closer to being on the other side of cancer treatment.

Personally, creativity became my ammunition. It is what energized me to wake up in the morning, and continues to do so to this day. It helped, and continues to help me harvest my imagination, reduce my anxiety, harbor my ideas and honor my fire and fuel.

Story Time

In this chapter, I want to share a story with you about how Alexa Curtis, who went from living in Mansfield, a small town in eastern Connecticut, to living in major cities, where she now lives what she calls "a life from a movie." She landed her first show on Radio Disney, *Fearless Everyday*, created the podcast *This is Life Unfiltered*, and wrote her own lifestyle and mental health blog. However, her success did not easily come to her. There was no fairy godmother who waved her magic wand and *poofed* her problems away like Cinderella.

Alexa's success was a result of her trauma. She struggled throughout her childhood with a devastating, life-altering event with her family. She took the courage to become the author of her own life, on her terms, despite her circumstances.

Alexa's story begins at a very young age. When she was seven, her father was wrongfully convicted of sexually assaulting a woman and put in maximum security prison in Princeton, Rhode Island.

"I would give up everything I have now to take that pain away from him."

It all started when he took a trip to a hotel where photos of a serial rapist were hanging behind the counter. Because her father had a similar appearance to the man in the photograph, somebody called the police on him, which soon led to his arrest. Fortunately, Alexa's father was diabetic, which prompted prosecutors to offer a plea bargain if he admitted guilt. By doing this, he avoided life in prison and was, instead, sentenced to four years in prison. Although his time in prison was decreased from the original forty-year sentence, Alexa still did not take it well.

It was hard. When I went to visit him, I was not allowed to see him for more than twenty minutes. For the first two years, I could not even see him alone. My mother had to be there. He had no freedom. Our relationship was so broken.

Not only did Alexa have to watch her father become isolated from his family but she also watched everyone close to her distance themselves. Alexa's mother suffered from severe depression after his arrest, her sister moved out to Staten Island, New York, and her classmates were too afraid to talk to her.

During this time, Alexa used the internet as a form of escape. She invested her free time into reading about fashion. This excited her, freed her from her despair, and transported her to a different world.

One day, Alexa was over at her sister's new home and showed her sister her favorite blog. It was *The Style Rookie*, a fashion blog started by writer, magazine editor, and actress Tavi Gevinson. Alexa's enthusiasm sparked an idea.

"You should start one," her sister said.

Alexa contemplated it for a while, but then searched "how to start a blog" on the internet. She found blogger. com, a free, easy-to-use blogging platform, and started *A Life in the Fashion Lane*. Alexa used this as a channel to express her creativity and explore her passion.

At the time I started it, I was not thinking anything of it; I just kept writing for myself. My blog was the only thing that I had. I had no friends. I was bullied in school, felt like I did not fit in because of my dad, and my parents were never around for me. Writing became my outlet, and to distract myself, I went online to my blogging community.

Little did she know, but at just twelve years old, she did something extraordinary. She planted a seed in a pot of soil that would blossom into a life she could never dream possible. This was the start of a new and extraordinary life.

From the ages of twelve to fifteen, she spent every bit of free time she had emailing bloggers, companies, and brands, pitching herself to land freelance writing gigs. During this time, she was freelance writing for *Parade* magazine and Guest of a Guest and was sent to New York to attend fashion shows.

After Alexa started to feel the euphoric effects from investing in her passion, she made the decision to start living for herself.

I put all of my energy into [blogging] and found that it was better to explore my own self. This is when I decided to drop out of my high school and transfer to an online school. This same day, I got a call from Rachel Ray's television show because they found my blog and wanted me to go on air.

I had no intention for [my blog] to become anything, but that day I knew I was making the right choice by finishing high school online. I put all of my energy and effort into what I loved, and I would suggest people also try something new because it helps in the long run.

The hobby Alexa used to escape from bullying turned into her side-hustle, and then into a job. At the age of seventeen, she moved to New York City, then Boston, and then Los Angeles. During her time in Manhattan, she found a passion for mental health and started to speak at high schools and at a conference led by Talkspace, an online therapy service.

Alexa went on to found Media Impact and Navigation for Teens, a nonprofit that helps empower young adults to find self-confidence through the power of public speaking. She focused more of her blog posts toward mental health and started to speak at various schools in Hartford, Connecticut, and at The British International *School* of *Boston* about these topics.

Over the next two years, she was a guest on television programs such as *Access Hollywood Live, Good Morning America,* and *Great Day Houston,* to name a few. She started to work with a talent manager, who helped catapult Alexa to her next agency, which then led her to be featured in a television segment on the morning show *CT Style,* where she started to get paid to speak on-air to talk about brands.

During this time, Alexa was offered a position with *Fearless Every Day,* a radio show on Radio Disney, to inspire other young adults to be their own person and follow their dreams. Not only did she run her show for one year but she also started her own podcast, *This is Life Unfiltered with Alexa Curtis*, where she talks to well-known entrepreneurs about how to live life "unfiltered."

Today, at just twenty-one years old, Alexa uses her passion as a platform to continue blogging about fashion full-time. She has shifted her focus to raising awareness on body positivity, on methods to deal with anxiety, on creating self-care practices, and on following your dreams from some of her favorite entrepreneurs such as Andy Puddicombe and Catt Sadler.

Not only does she shine through her career but she also draws on the hardship of her father's incarceration as inspiration to live each day to the fullest. She is inspired by his efforts to live each day to the fullest and remain positive despite the odds being stacked against him. Because of this, she has gotten involved in the Innocence Project, an organization that helps free innocent people who are incarcerated.

Action Plan and Lesson

Pursuing her dreams gave her an experience Alexa never anticipated. She looked up to people who inspired her to persevere fearlessly. Alexa gives the following advice:

Every time something bad happens, it should not determine your destiny. Don't compare yourself to anyone. It is better to be your own person, get out of your comfort zone, and try something new.

Explore what you like, and put everything into it to distract yourself. Realize that [your struggle] is just 'right now' and not forever. Ask yourself what you really want to do. If pursuing what you do makes you happy and is benefiting you, it will be okay.

You have two paths in life and it is up to you to decide, that regardless of what happens to you, which route you want to go down. You can take what happened to you, embrace it, and move onto the next.

With that, I would suggest that you ask yourself what you enjoy doing. William C. Menninger, M.D., says that "hobbies are recognized as being of benefit to the mental health of the individual and consequently of importance to civilian morale.. [they] do furnish an individual a release of and relaxation from tension." If this is the case, then what are you waiting for? Make a list and number them in order, identifying which ones make you the most joyful. Afterward, explore the ways you could incorporate your pleasures into your day-to-day life. When you invest your time into the things you enjoy, unexpected benefits may unfold before your eyes.

Reflect

How will you infuse a spark into your soul?

Chapter 6

Pushing through Limits with an Open Mind

You have to lift your head up out of the mud and just do it.

—TERI GARR

It is evident that when we experience a troubling emotion or are faced with an upsetting crisis, we feel like there is no possible way to get ourselves out of it. Maybe we think it is unattainable to reclaim our physical health after falling off-track from our mundane routine. Or we may think it is beyond possible to get hired again after being unemployed or losing a job. And for more serious circumstances, maybe we think walking after breaking our leg or recovering from a serious operation is impossible.

This is all imposter syndrome. We are just being too hard on ourselves. How could we know what we can actually achieve if we do not at least try?

For instance, before embarking on my book writing journey, I did not think that it was possible. I had never heard of anyone my age revealing both this much personal information and wisdom to the world in the form of literature. I thought I had to have had many more years of life experience to be where I am today like Eckhart Tolle and Oprah Winfrey.

Whenever I had these thoughts, I reminded myself that everyone's journey is different and age does not justify experience. There are people my age who have gone through worse ordeals that I cannot relate to. And on the contrary, there are also those who have not been through any trauma at all.

One of the people who helped me realize this was Jay Shetty, a viral content creator and award-winning storyteller. Here is a little bit on Jay's story.

Jay recognized that he wanted to escape his unfulfilled life working in the corporate world and learn how to live a life of simplicity and gratitude; like the monk he shadowed during his free time after his corporate nine to five work job, he jumped into something new. Jay was able to see the possibility of the unimaginable and devoted three years of his life to the monastic world.

In short, after leaving the monastery, Jay had a hard time jumping back into society again. He felt disconnected and unaccepted. He was rejected by forty companies who would have hired him before he became a monk, and he was conflicted about how to go forward with his life. He was stressed and put under pressure. Was joining the monastery the right move, or had it been a mistake? Was the setback impossible to overcome?

At the same time, Jay identified something interesting in his friends at work. In the same way Jay was stressing out about entering the workforce again, he saw his friends emotionally suffering from their jobs. They were depleted and burned out, and Jay would console them with the lessons he learned in his three years as a monk. He positively changed their perspectives.

The positive feedback Jay received from his friends influenced him to start teaching CEOs and other executives about meditation, wellness, and health—all pillars he focused on during his dedication to ministry.

Jay's purpose started to unleash itself before his eyes. He was catapulted into a new life, and he started to persevere. He was first called to join the monastery, engaged himself full-force into practice, and then started to incorporate his teachings in other people's lives. He was implementing his deep-rooted spiritual knowledge with others versus the one he used to live by committing himself to something that was out of the ordinary.

Today, Jay is an icon. He pushed through what he thought to be his limits and has escalated the lives of other individuals on a large scale. He has been featured in *Forbes, National Geographic*, and on the BBC, to name a few; he has hosted conferences and had speaking engagements at large companies like Google and L'Oréal, coaches celebrities, runs a podcast, and has gained 4 billion views and more than 24 million followers on his social platforms.

He says that "You can't be who you can't see, and so if you've never seen someone do anything, you'll never think that 'I can do it.'" The only way you can make your dreams possible is if you are the one who tries. You need to set that goal, make a plan, believe in yourself, and follow through in order to persevere.

Story Time

It is important to go into things with an open mind because chances are you can meet someone who will model it for you. It can be frustrating to jump into something new, but you truly never know who you will meet and what path they will take you on next, which, interestingly enough, links back to two chapters ago.

Something similar happened to Jack Wallace, a US gold medalist Paralympian from New Jersey. At the age of ten, Jack was in a water-skiing accident during the summertime on Lake George after he was pulled underneath a boat by its propeller.

"I was shocked, in pain, and was fading in and out of consciousness. I thought to myself, 'I am dying,'" he said.

Jack was put into an ambulance and woke up to trauma: he lost part of his right leg. It had been amputated, and there was nothing he could do about it.

Jack stayed in the hospital until the end of the summer, and by Thanksgiving, he received his first prosthetic. Finally, after he was given the opportunity to walk again, all he wanted to do was take his rollerblades out and skate in the driveway. Courageous and fearless, he strapped his feet into his blades and tried to jump back into the way he used to skate without his prosthetic, but he fell every time.

I got frustrated. I shut down and even stopped watching my favorite sport, [which was] hockey. Hockey got me through the time I spent in the hospital, but I thought I was not going to ever be able to do anything for the rest of my life like this again. Sports were my whole life and I wanted to continue playing, but it felt impossible.

During this time of despair, Jack's family discovered the organization Camp No Limits, which is for kids dealing with limb loss. That next summer, Jack's life changed. He learned of a new way that hockey could be part of his life. He was inspired to incorporate hockey in his life again. He was very upset for a time, but he was able to overcome his battle with the new support group around him.

The first day I saw a kid with no arms throwing a Frisbee and football with a perfect spiral. This was my pivotal moment that I knew I should not feel sorry for myself and I can push through. Being around these kids made me realize that this is not a limitation. [Camp] gave me a new perspective and showed me that [my leg] would not be a limitation.

After that summer was over, Jack found a local hockey team he could play with. Woodbridge Warriors became his outlet. "I fell in love with the sport all over again," he said.

One of his teammates, Josh Pauls, inspired Jack to do something larger with his life. Josh was a double above-the-knee amputee and went to the 2010 Winter Paralympics and won the gold. Jack saw the pinnacle of the sport through his teammate and made it his goal to strive for gold as well.

At age eleven, Jack took it upon himself to strive for his dreams. He kept surrounding himself with others who were involved in ice hockey. The following year, he played at the junior level in hockey and got invited to the US Development Camp run by USA Hockey, where coaches scouted for potential players to recruit for the national team. At the age of thirteen, Jack was able to play for a team in an adult league, and a year later, at fourteen, he made the US National Development team.

In 2016, he moved to the National Team, won a silver medal in a tournament in Gangneung, South Korea, and was then named to the US Paralympic team. On March 17, 2018, he finally won the gold in Pyeongchang. Jack continues to play on the US National Team, which was recently deemed the 2019 Para Ice Hockey World Champions. Today, Jack gives back to his community in the same way Jay coaches others. Jack has been a mentor to children at Camp No Limits and attends benefits at nonprofit organizations and various foundations.

Action Plan and Lesson

If Jack did not see the possibility of playing hockey again, he would have never been able to have the opportunity to live up to what was most important to him. The main takeaway from Jack's story is that engaging in activities outside your comfort zone can be beneficial for you in the long-run. This is why, despite your battle, you need to have faith in yourself and your dreams, and keep an open mind.

Understand two things: you are capable of changing your life, and you are strong enough to have the courage to reach a goal and pursue a dream. If someone else is doing it, you can do it too.

Let's say you enjoy baking. You decide to take a baking class, then you are inspired to become a certified baker, start a YouTube channel and blog, gain a bunch of views, and open your own shop and store. You may embark on a journey that you have never seen done before, kind of like Jack Witherspoon, a three-time leukemia survivor.

When Witherspoon was undergoing treatment at six years old, he discovered a love for cooking. He took this passion to a new level. After hosting a cooking event at a local restaurant to raise money for charity, local news channels, cooking shows, and the press started to become interested in his passions. He was featured on Jay Leno's *The Tonight Show* and on the Food Network, and then wrote *Twist It Up: More Than 60 Delicious Recipes from an Inspiring Young Chef.* And he did this all when he was a young child.

At the age of eighteen, he created Skonies, a dessert that's a combination of a cookie and scone, which is available at UCLA Medical Center and Miller Children's Hospital. He took his love for baking and created something that most adults do not even pursue. How amazing is that? Dream BIG!

The world is your oyster. You never know how the next chapter of your life will open up for you. Use your interests to ultimately help you persevere in life.

Reflect

What kind of person are you striving to be, and how will you change?

Chapter 7

Vulnerability as a Virtue

To share your weakness is to make yourself vulnerable; to make yourself vulnerable is to show your strength.

—CRISS JAMI

Can we get an Amen? Do you agree with Criss? I surely do!

A lot of people would agree that becoming vulnerable is like showing your weakness. What those people do not understand is that it takes a lot of strength and courage to show your true self. It might be one of the most difficult phenomena, but when you express your innermost self, there is no stress. You free yourself from the proverbial weight on your shoulders.

While undergoing treatment, I realized that the more I started to accept my situation and open up to people about it, I not only started to feel comfortable and welcomed but I also realized that people would reciprocate back. They would share similar stories, allowing me to feel less alone in this battle, like with Mike earlier.

I experienced this sense of camaraderie one afternoon at a local store. My cashier complimented me on my buzz cut. I was flattered and accepted her compliment with grace. As I accepted my receipt and started to gather my bags to leave, she continued to speak to me. She shared with me that she also had her head buzzed. "I lost all of my hair to breast cancer over twenty years ago," she said. I paused and looked at her.

She was my light of hope at that moment. The fact that she was standing alive to this day, cancer-free, made me start to tear up. There was something that motivated me to share my story with her on why my head was buzzed.

She inspired me to take pride in my flaw, to become vulnerable. I told her that my hairstyle was not by choice, but rather because I had cancer and was currently undergoing chemotherapy.

She started to share with me the beauty of coming out on the other side, and encouraged me to keep my faith high because I was going to be okay. At the same time, another woman overheard the conversation and came up to us. She shared with me that she also had cancer.

We became friends, and she gifted me the tools that got her through her fight, one being *Power Thoughts: 365 Daily Affirmations* by Louise L. Hay, an inspirational self-help book. From this experience, I learned that when you become vulnerable, people will connect with you. Others may have a similar story, or know of someone who is in your shoes. There are more people in your position than you know. When you put yourself out there, you will find others in your shoes, and they can help you propel and persevere. As actress Angela Robinson would say, "The world is such a small place."

Story Time

During her freshman year of college, Hannah (name changed for a request for anonymity) felt alone in the transition into her new chapter in life. She did not know how to adjust to this new way of living. She was afraid that she was going to experience the same emotions she did in high school, where she did not feel like she fit in socially.

She was frustrated, but as she started to open up to her peers about her anxiety, she noticed that everyone was also having a difficult time adjusting to college, not just her.

The day that changed my perspective was when I was sitting in the library on a Wednesday night. I felt overwhelmed as I was studying for a test. I was just staring at my book, about to cry. This one random girl, who I had never seen before in my life, sat next to me, stopped what she was doing, and turned over to ask me if everything was okay.

She asked me, 'Do you want to talk about how you are feeling? I can tell you seem stressed.'

I talked to her a little, and then she opened up to me about how she was also feeling really stressed and overwhelmed. It was a short conversation, but it, overall, made me feel like there was a community at school. It was comforting, and just the fact that she stopped what she was doing to ask about me was so nice.

It made me feel like people were looking out for me, even people I did not even know. Now, I do the same and encourage others to as well. People assume they are the only ones suffering, but they are not. When you feel alone, that can make it even worse, but no one is ever alone.

Hannah was inspired by this incident to create change on campus. She started to ask others in her classes and dormitory hall if they felt anxious as well. She discovered that they were also restless. What could she do to change this? She wanted to be a supportive friend, the same way the student was for her in the library.

Hannah was inspired to get involved in numerous programs on her campus, including a counseling program where she was trained to become a counselor for those in need. After this program, she started to fill in the white space at her school by bringing more mental health awareness services to campus. One of the things Hannah was able to request was to set up an educational program to train organizations on campus that had to handle serious situations that require emotional aid, such as Emergency Medical Services (EMS). This had a lot of success.

Some patients complained that they did not feel a connection with the EMS team on an emotional level. This is why I initiated a plan to help fill this gap. We developed a program to help train EMS to be more empathetic and patient.

This started to fuel me to become even more involved on campus. After this, I then started to participate in a mental health organization. We specifically tried to target freshmen because of how we all felt when we were new students. I was the outreach chair for our programs. I hosted a lot of meditation and bamboo planting events.

We engaged in little projects. Before people have exams, we stayed outside the room and gave out candy or gave little papers with jokes on them to lift up their spirits. We also hosted a spa night on campus to help people to relax.

Awareness of mental health on campus has really grown because of my team's work. We changed the conversation and made emotions more inclusive. People did not really talk about mental health issues [like anxiety and depression] my freshman year, but now people are more open to talking about it. We even hung up posters on campus with encouraging quotes from students' experiences with mental health.

During her junior year, Hannah was inspired to start a social media campaign where she interviewed students, faculty, and anyone within the university's community about their struggles.

We ended up getting a lot of positive feedback. We had about 100 participants the first semester—it was such a surprise to see how many people were willing to share their personal stories with our community! We had one professor share his useful insights and one student who shared how he overcame his social anxiety on campus due to his struggle with having autism. One international student reached out and appreciated how we were trying to change that in our school setting and let others know that they are not alone.

Action Plan and Lesson

It is quite amazing how one small encounter at the library turned into a larger movement. Hannah continues to encourage others to open up about their struggles, even out of college. She thinks that it is important for people to know that there are communities out there. She suggests to even use social media as your platform.

"Start posting things that you feel passionate about, and maybe other people will follow. You have to be patient. You are not alone," she says.

For anyone who is looking to help others, Hannah suggests starting conversations. Here are her steps:

1. Ask a person in need if they would like to talk.
2. Allow them to come up with feeling-words, like "stressed," on their own.
3. Ask them to talk more about that feeling.
4. Lastly, validate their feelings and tell them that it is understandable.

Sometimes we can associate vulnerability with a lack of control or power, but it actually displays great grit. It gives us an opportunity to turn something heavy into something light and manageable. Our secrets can become a sanctuary of safety for others, and our panics can help unleash our passions.

Do not be afraid to ask someone if they are okay and share your story. Be brave and bold and know that your story can help others persevere.

Reflect

What's holding you back from becoming vulnerable?

How can you become vulnerable?

Chapter 8

Believe in the Unimaginable

Belief produces the acceptance of existence. That is why you can believe what no one else thinks is true. It is true for you because it was made by you.

—A COURSE IN MIRACLES

Belief is defined as "a state or habit of mind in which trust or confidence is placed in some person or thing," according to *Merriam-Webster Dictionary*. When you are confident in something, you become certain. When you are certain, you are undoubtedly calm. Without trust, we do not have the power to be calm.

During the remainder of 2017, it was tough for me to be relaxed. I did not think I was going to get better in the timeframe the doctors set because my overbearing fatigue and queasiness took control of my mood. I had forgotten what it felt like to be healthy. And on top of that, my hair kept falling out in clumps. This made me insecure (as you may remember from the previous chapters).

I started to develop a victim mentality. Because I was seeing my appearance change right before my eyes, I believed I was dying. Cancer took away the Alexa I knew and left me staring at the reflection of a stranger in the mirror.

With courage, I remembered the reason I lost control of my appearance. It was because I was actually getting healthy. The toxicity of chemotherapy was working, and the cancer cells within me were slowly dying from the poison. Reversing my judgment allowed me to embrace my bald head. This was my opportunity to let the world know that I was a fighter.

Shortly after, I decided to walk to a local barbershop to shave off my remaining locks. "I need to get a buzz cut," I told the manager. Puzzled and in shock, he sat me down in a chair. "I am going through chemotherapy and started to lose my hair, so I need you to shave off everything," I said. I started to feel empowered. A little while later, I walked out onto the streets of Manhattan confidently sporting my newly bald head.

Because I changed my initial insecure beliefs, I began to persevere. I felt like a rock star with conviction. I started to collect photos of women who rocked my hairstyle to inspire me to believe that I could also rock it as well. I made this an opportunity to have fun with my new appearance. I wore more makeup than usual and tons of jewelry. I wanted to look chic like Amber Rose and bold like Jessie J.

Story Time

Sometimes what we think sets the groundwork for how we live. Instead of feeling sorry for myself when I started to lose all of my hair, I took it as an opportunity to lift my spirits and find the positive. Another extraordinary example of someone who lives like this is Grace Wethor, an actress, dancer, and model from Minnesota.

In seventh grade, Grace became ill. She was very tired and unmotivated to do the things she loved. It was unlike her. She was outgoing and full of life, and now she was unambitious and dull. She knew something was wrong.

The moment it changed was the day of one of my dance com petitions. I did not want to go [to the competition], although

I had been training for it for years. This was the day my mom took me into the emergency room.

She thought I might have mono, so they did a blood test. From this they discovered my red and white blood cells were off and my B-12 levels were very high. I was sent to the hematology department because the doctors thought I might have leukemia, but I did not. I was sent home.

For six months, I was still tired. I was told I had depression, but I knew that was not the case. The doctors finally did an MRI after I complained of a headache. That day, I was diagnosed with a brain stem glioma, a brain tumor in the pons. I was given an 8 percent survival rate for the upcoming six months.

It was a long journey to get to the diagnosis, and although it was not good, everyone was happy because it was such a struggle to figure out what was wrong. There was no treatment for my tumor as opposed to starting chemotherapy in two days or having surgery in five hours [like other types of cancer].

The moment I was diagnosed, I told the doctors, '[This] is ridiculous; I am going to live.'

[At this time], my mom first sat me down and said, 'We need to evaluate every part of your life because things are going to change; there's nothing you can do about that, but the way you decide to change each individual part of your life is very important.'

Grace was unable to understand why she was diagnosed. She was always active and ate healthy every day, just like me. At the time of her diagnosis, she was facing a variety of mixed emotions. She did not know what was happening or what was going to happen and sat in silence the first initial week.

The one thing Grace did know was that her life was worth living. Grace looked at the person she was before her diagnosis, and looked at the things that she always wanted to pursue. Cancer was not going to stop her. And after all, it was just a word. She viewed her diagnosis as something positive and something that pushed her to do things beyond her beliefs.

I did not want to live in a hospital because it was only going to make me feel worse. [My diagnosis] propelled me. I grew up in the circus and in performing arts and knew what I loved before I was diagnosed. The diagnosis was a moment for me to push myself and pursue my dreams full-force. I could not just sit back and wait for things to happen. I said, 'Okay, I am doing this.'

The week after her diagnosis, she made the choice to move to Los Angeles to pursue acting and modeling. She realized life was too short and she needed to do what was going to make her happy and cancer was not going to control her. Just after Grace shifted her focus on what gave her joy, she hit the six-month survival rate.

Grace then hit a year, and now she is over four years past the original diagnosis. This remarkable news inspired her to become an active member in the cancer community by attending benefits and events hosted by foundations in order to raise awareness to help other young cancer patients around her.

She was invited to the United Nations to discuss its 17 Sustainable Development Goals about youth health and well-being. She never thought this was possible, but she was able to turn it into a reality.

She attended Camp Mak-A-Dream, a center where cancer survivors and family members can connect and talk. Grace has attended this camp for three years and has made some of the best friends in her life. The thing she enjoys most is being able to see how much they have all grown together.

Although it can look like her life is in a state of bliss, it is not all fun and games. Grace knows that her situation could be worse. Grace has the knowledge that if her tumor had spread, it could have caused half of her face to be completely paralyzed.

At times, it is scary. When I go back to the hospital, it hits me. I tell myself, 'You have to remember it could just be something that is there forever, but you have to strive to be the best you can be no matter your current situation.'

[Anyone] can make plans and think [they] have everything figured out, but you really never know. You have to take it day by day, and that is okay. There are endless things that can happen in your life, and you just have to look at it in the 'now.' You shouldn't compare yourself to others because it is a different journey for everyone.

Although Grace has small periods of discomfort, she reminds herself that she needs to be thankful for how much she has accomplished already. She believes that her attitude of gratitude helps her get up each morning and can help others as well.

Even Deepak Chopra, a pioneer in integrative medicine and personal development, says that *"Gratitude is good for you; it creates a biochemical shift in the body. The brain responds to positive input and sends life-enhancing messages to every cell."* With that, it is clear that looking at the positive things and being an optimist can give the strength to anyone to keep on fighting through their storm.

If Grace had decided to listen to her doctors, believed that she was going to die, and continued to live in a hospital, then she would have never lived a fulfilled life nor been able to achieve all of her accomplishments. Her push to purpose allowed her to travel all around the world for her career, give TED Talks, walk the runways of New York Fashion Week, and work with *Teen Vogue, Elle, Harper's Bazaar,* and Pink by Victoria's Secret. She even wrote the book *You're So Lucky* to discuss the unconventional life of teens with cancer. Grace believes her story is universally important and wants to inspire others to pursue their aspirations no matter their situation or illness.

For those going through an illness, Grace suggests the following:

Evaluate who you are without the sickness and how you can incorporate the sickness into what you love. Find what makes you feel good outside of your diagnosis.

Action Plan and Lesson

All in all, life is unpredictable: you do not know what will happen tomorrow. When circumstances test you, know that it is okay to challenge the rules. Even if some things are impossible or seem to be unattainable, it is important to at least try to set goals for yourself. They can help you reach milestones just like they helped Grace. She made it a goal to pursue modeling, and she achieved it.

An easy way to do this is to make a vision board, similar to the photos I gathered after I got my hair shaved. During treatment, my mother gifted me *Dream It. Pin It. Live It* by Terri Savelle Foy. In this book, Terri talks about how you can manifest your fantasies into reality by creating a vision board. It was my dream to feel confident, and surrounding myself with photos of females who embodied this gave me the ability to feel like my old self. Terri defines a vision board as:

A collage of pictures and images...[that] range from aspirations you want to achieve and your deepest desires in fulfilling your personal life goals...

The images you visualize in your mind become your reality. Your mind is like a magnet. Whatever gets in your mind and stays there, you will attract in your life...

Your thoughts are a pathway to your destiny. Your life today is a reflection of the dominating thoughts you allowed to take up residence in your mind yesterday.

My mother wanted me to use this book as a spark of hope and inspiration, to manifest and create. And it sure did work. After I read it, I became inspired to create one of my own. It was an opportunity to distract myself and let my imagination run free. I started to believe in the unimaginable possibilities that life had in store for me.

In fact, I still have a photo of mine hanging by my bedroom cabinet. I pasted photos of destinations I wished to visit, images of healthy meals that were going to help me heal, people exercising and staying fit, old college photos with my friends, and things that were beyond my wildest dreams on a piece of paper. And yes, writing a book was on that board! Who knew I was going to be doing it so soon.

Guess what? I was able to manifest all of these things and more. I was presented with an opportunity to travel with my father on a work-related trip. I asked my oncologist if it would be okay for me to fly at this point, being that I had ended treatment only a few weeks prior. Based on all the recent blood work results, he gave me the okay. He encouraged me to return back to how I was living my life before the disease, but of course, to maintain a healthy lifestyle. Therefore, I embraced the opportunity and not only did I travel to Arizona, but I also then traveled with him to California and Bermuda.

Later, I was able to continue my undergraduate degree and reclaim my health through food and fitness, allowing me to ride with Cycle for Survival with a group of friends. I was mysteriously blessed to have been able to have these events happen in my life, and it was all because I believed in them. With this, I encourage you to post images of things that will inspire you to manifest in your life. Believe they can happen, and maybe they will.

Reflect

What is one thing you view as negative in your life at the moment, and how can you positively change its outcome?

What dreams of yours do you want to become true?

Chapter 9

Rise Above It All with Help from God

The most important thing is God's blessing and if you believe in God and you believe in yourself, you have nothing to worry about.

—MOHAMED AL-FAYED

I hope after reading the last chapter you were able to take action and proactively start to fulfill your dreams. In this chapter, I want to inspire you to seek God in doing so because of how much I have seen him change my life. I am sure you realized how important God is to me from the beginning of this book. You will learn more about why he became so important to me in the next chapter. First, I would like to share with you how he helped me persevere through the pain I felt during chemotherapy.

Before I started treatment, several of my friends and family members would reassure me that I was going to come out a stronger person, that I was going to grow so much from this next stage in my life. Quite honestly, I was not sure if they were telling me this because they did not know what else to say, or if they could truly attest to this claim.

The involuntary feeling of fear that grew inside me overshadowed anything that seemed to look positive. However, there was a little part of me that wanted to believe them. It was only when I spoke to my Aunt Ro that I began to think differently. She told me, "God would not put things in your life he did not think you would be able to handle." That encouragement was enough to help lift my spirits.

I can truly assure you that the vitality I received from this battle has changed me a way that I still cannot fully put into words to this day. I found that because I trusted in God, I was given his strength to persevere. If I did not try to grasp onto the little courage left in me, and pray to God every day, I would not be here today.

I compare this to the analogy of a tulip bulb being planted into soil and blossoming into a bright yellow flower. Or to the parable of the mustard seed in the

Bible from Matthew 13:31–32: "Though it is the smallest of all seeds, yet when it grows, it is the largest of garden plants and becomes a tree, so that the birds come and perch in its branches." Or to what the ancient Greek father of tragedy, Aeschylus, said: "From a small seed a mighty trunk may grow." Whether it is a flower or tree, after something is planted, it will grow. Just like you: once you plant a seed in God, he will start to bless you in little ways.

Story Time

During the same time I was getting stronger, Wes Woodson, an old friend of mine, was also experiencing a moment of growth. One evening, Wes made a post on his Instagram account with the caption "didn't really want to write about this...but I figured if I'm going to put my story out there, I can't do it halfway. Link in bio," directing his followers to a blog post on Medium.com titled "I Am Leopard Boy..." about the new clothing line he started, the hidden. I was curious about learning more on his story, so I gave him a call. What was supposed to be a brief chat ended up turning into a two-hour conversation of Wes walking me through every moment that led him to this point.

Wes's journey began at the age of twelve. He was taken by surprise by what he thought was a minor accident while he was playing basketball with his friends. "I was trying to imitate Michael Jordan and make a free throw, but I fell flat on the ground and cut myself," he said.

As his wound on his knee started to heal, white dots around the open part of the wound started to appear. Weeks later, he noticed the same dots on his hands and feet. He was worried, but did not think anything major of it. After he brought this to his parents' attention, they went to the doctor. Here, Wes was informed that he had a lifetime disease. Wes was diagnosed with vitiligo, a skin condition that affects the loss of pigmentation in the skin, and there was nothing he could do about it.

I felt like I lost my identity. Not only was I one of the only colored kids in my town, now I had this condition that made me stick out more.

I was constantly bullied. I was too black for the white kids and too white for the black kids. I felt like I did not belong. I did not fit in, and felt like I was not worthy enough. I had nobody, and low and behold, I was diagnosed with an auto-immune disease called vitiligo that made me half white and half black.

By the end of that summer, Wes had spots on his hands, feet, and around his mouth. Within just two months, his appearance completely changed. He looked like a different person, and it was all out of his control. When he started sixth grade that year, his friends noticed the difference and students started to call him everything from "Michael Jackson" and "Oreo" to "Leopard Boy."

During my junior year of high school, I began to realize that worrying about it was a waste of time, and that I was giving people way too much power over what they thought of me. I realized that it was really hurting my self-confidence, and I started to develop social anxiety.

Then, I took it upon myself to say, 'Hey, I have two options. I can change my attitude or let the spots define who I am.' I decided to change my attitude. Then I created a concept in my mind to start a mission to encourage others to not feel the way I did. I wanted to promote this mission of being your true self. It took me eight years to get to this point.

I realized I was not the only one who did this, like Malala Yousafzai, a Pakistani girl who fights for the rights of women pursuing education. A little background about her, she was in twelfth grade, the Taliban raided her village and made everything illegal from books and music, to the right for women to pursue an education.

As a response, Malala spoke out, but was shot her in the head. After long surgeries and recovery to survive, she realized she could allow this to define her whole future or change her mindset and use being shot as fuel to fight for education. She chose the second and now inspires millions of people, and even won a Noble Peace Prize. She only did so by embracing change.

Even Inky Johnson, an all-star football player from the University of Tennessee. He thought that he was going to go first-round draft pick to the NFL, but during his last college football game, he took a hard hit, causing his whole right arm to become instantly paralyzed. Today he inspires others to embrace change in their daily life. I believe Malala and Inky were on to something. They each showed us that the only way we can really confront change is through embracing in it. This makes us multidimensional and unique.

It all started at a summer camp when my friend Eli asked me a personal question during our bathroom break. He single-handedly changed my perspective after he asked me, 'What's up with your hands?' I froze, trying to find a reasonable explanation, but before I thought of anything to say, Eli said that my spots were cool and made me look 'unique' as he walked away. In that moment, I started to accept my disease.

I remember walking out of that bathroom with my a chest a little higher, and my hands out of my pockets. I felt proud to have them. I was able to accept that my spots were a part of who I am and what makes me, me.

And after I made that blog post on Medium, one of my friends told me that it helped his mother, who also had vitiligo, get out of her depression. I also saw people I did not know wearing my hoodies from the hidden around my college campus at Babson, supporting my movement. It was only the beginning, and I was inspired to continue to open up about my story. It built my character.

Things happen for a reason, and I only praise God more for it because without this, I don't think I would be in this position that I am in today.

I actually had an encounter like this. One of the scariest moments of my life was the day of my first PET/CT scan, which was going to determine which stage of cancer I had and how much chemotherapy I would have to receive. I could have stage 1 and receive two months of chemo, or stage 4 and almost a year of chemo.

Before the scan, the nurses took me down the hall to a small room on the right. All that was in the room was a chair and a small table with several needles, liquid injections to prep for the scan, saline, and bandages. A nurse secured the IV in my arm with a clear bandage and injected contrast and isotope into the vein of my left arm. She told me that she would come back in forty-five minutes and then closed the door behind her.

The only two things left in the room were me and the chair. I started to have a panic attack as the fear inside of me grew larger and larger. I honestly did not want to be doing this.

I did not know what else to do, so I asked God for help. All of a sudden, a wave of calmness casted over my body, and the tears streaming down my face stopped. I had a feeling that I was going to be okay, that I had to go through this battle for a reason. I said, 'God, I am going to do this for you,' and at that moment I started to truly place my trust in something greater than me.

Before the hidden, I was sent to a week-long leadership conference in Nova Scotia, Canada, at St. Francis Xavier University. The basis of this conference was on getting in touch with your inner self. I was out of my comfort zone, but at the end, I believe God opened my eyes to my gift, the gift of public speaking.

The last night of the week conference, we had a talent show. I did not want to do it because I did not believe I was talented, but one of my friends encouraged me to say the monologue "Not Poor, Just Broke" by Dick Gregory, which was about a black boy who got racially profiled by his teacher. After I recited it, one of the counselors was brought to tears.

It was not the fact that she cried in my arms that I knew 'I am doing this for you, God,' but it was more so that by her crying I realized I had been ignoring the gifts that God gave me. If someone I had never met in my life was so touched by something that I did not think was a gift, I felt like I was doing God a great disservice.

At that moment, I knew I was put on this earth to inspire through no matter what I did, clothing, or business, as long as I followed that vision of seeking out to inspire people, that's when I knew I was doing it for God.

I learned that there are three layers to understand every problem. Ask yourself these three questions:

1. What is bothering me?
2. How is it bothering me?
3. Why is it bothering me? This one is the deepest and hardest part.

In this case, my white spots were bothering me because people would laugh at me, and it bothered me because I was confused on who I was; I was insecure. After doing this exercise, I learned that I cannot please everyone, but focus on the most important people around me and the man upstairs.

I do not even question if I am supposed to be in this class or in this room [at school right now]. It is in believing God put me here for a reason that I feel like I am a more complete person.

My relationship with God is making me feel like I am a more wholesome person. I was very confused when I was a child. I had anger issues, and not any means at peace with who I am today.

Action Plan and Lesson

At the end of our conversation, Wes told me one last thing: "The only way we can confront change is by embracing it." I realized that Wes and I were both able to confront our change by embracing our agony. We both turned to God in times of need to give us strength.

Wes got to where he is today because he was trusting his life in someone else's hands. He has been able to see how this has positively affected his life as he is now doing public speaking events at local high schools and even had the opportunity to present "What We Do When Faced with Change" at TEDx Babson College. He even has his own YouTube channel called WesDaily.

There is truly something greater out there that we can all follow to help us through our battles. It is not until we look inward and ask for help that we will receive it. Honor your battle and use God's strength to get you through. Pray to him and ask him to help you, and he will. In the next chapter, you will learn more about how to use God's grace through faith to help you persevere.

Reflect

What is one thing you would ask God to help you conquer?

Chapter 10

Have Faith in a Higher Power

No matter what has happened to you in the past or what is going on in your life right now, it has no power to keep you from having an amazingly good future if you will walk by faith in God.

—*JOYCE MEYER*

Now that you have had a glimpse of God's grace, I want to encourage you to have faith. Faith is a very special gift. It is trust in something, or someone, greater. Martin Luther, an influential figure during the Protestant Reformation, defines faith as "a living, daring confidence in God's grace, so sure and certain that a man could stake his life on it a thousand times." Just like Luther, I place my faith in God. He is always available for us to turn toward as a divine option. The reason I believe this to be true is because of the relationship I built with him through my traumatic experience.

Believing in a higher power, like God, is what helps me get through each day. Whenever I feel alone, God allows me to escape that isolation and make me feel like I have a companion. However, there are times where we question the divine. When all your prospects are bleak, it is very common to lose faith. Perhaps your circumstance is hope-filled, but you begin to lose this sense of encouragement because of the projected anguish that will come with the experience.

I was entangled with this experience mostly after cancer. Although I am told that the recurrence of my cancer is extremely slim, I still battle with the thought of it coming back. I am afraid of undergoing such horrible agony again. It is precisely at this intersection where faith becomes most important.

When I come to these terms, I remind myself that God does not challenge me with difficulties he does not think I could handle, regardless of how horrible they make me feel. In general, troubling times are God's way of bringing us in closer to his comfort. He uses your hardships as vessels to trusting him. God has made a pathway for our lives, and it is up to us to have faith in him.

We must remember that the mystery of life and the struggles we go through have a message behind them. They are not the *end*, but rather the beginning of a new chapter. You just need to believe in something larger to get you through your struggle in order to persevere.

If the path was just easy, we'd forget to call on something greater than us. We'd just rely on our own limited power, and we wouldn't need to open to God and Course, this amazing energy that we are a part of.

—Jenny Hogg Ashwell

The reason I believe in faith so much is because of a very unique memory I experienced before cancer. I share this story with you to inspire you to believe in a greater universal power. This all happened when I was just seventeen years old. I visited a place that I identify as heaven. Perhaps you may refer to it as the Promised Land, New Jerusalem, the City of God, or the Kingdom of Heaven. Funny enough, although I was raised to believe that this is where you go once you die, I did not die when I saw it. I actually thought heaven was all a hoax until I experienced it myself. No one I knew had ever told me about an encounter they had in heaven besides my grandfather just before he woke from his coma.

At exactly 5:37 a.m. on an ordinary Tuesday morning, my eyes opened wide. I gasped for air, and my heart started to race. Everything I had just experienced was so realistic that I had to literally pinch myself to make sure I was still alive. I ran to my desk to grab paper and pen to write down what I just experienced so I wouldn't forget. Moments before I awoke, I was in a blank white space. Within seconds, I was struck by a bright light coming from the upper right side. As I focused my attention there, I noticed this light had a rectangular shape, outlined in a gold metal glowing frame. All of a sudden, the light coming from this space was growing brighter and brighter, so I squinted my eyes, then shut them completely, and turned my head to the left because I was blinded by some presence I couldn't quite define. Before I could understand what was happening to me, I felt someone's hand touch my right shoulder. It warmed my soul. I looked down at the hand, which was protruding out of a white cotton, linen-like sleeve, and then felt an arm around my back as if I was being hugged. I slowly turned my head to the left and looked up to identify the face. Glowing next to me was a man with light-colored eyes and dark brown hair.

Before I was able to identify who this gentleman was, I heard the words, "Do not worry, everything is going to be okay," echoing from a distance in a deep voice. Instantly, I woke up! I had just experienced another reality. Of course, once I put all the pieces together that morning, I was able to recognize that the man speaking to me was Jesus Christ, and I was standing in front of the golden gates of heaven. But to be completely honest with you, I have no idea how I ended up there. I do not think I necessarily died, but I do think a little part inside me needed to be saved. I was under a lot of additional stress because it was days before I was supposed to submit my college applications. I thought this was going to determine the rest of my life, which, in fact, it did not. However, I do believe this was a memory planted into my brain and heart for a time such as this.

So faith comes from hearing, and hearing through the word of Christ.

—Romans 10:17

I revisited the moment for the first time again a little over two years later, when I was overwhelmed with my cancer. I reminded myself that there was more to life because I had already been to the other side. I remembered there was something bigger out there, and I am only having a temporary human experience. All I can think of now is perhaps my encounter was a sign to me that whatever was going to come in my life, I needed to trust all would be okay because there is more to life than we experience here on Earth. This one moment was my personal catalyst that caused me to shift my energy and faith and opened my eyes to a greater power and the magic of the universe.

Story Time

Rex Duval, hereinafter known as PR, is the pastor and founder of Prison in the Wild, a registered nondenominational 501(c)(3) that facilitates Christian-focused life coaching to men and women on the streets, as well as in prisons. PR and I were both saved through the grace of God, only we experienced different circumstances. I gave PR a call and asked him to share his story and wisdom.

He grew up in a toxic environment. At twelve, his father introduced him to cocaine. This destroyed the innocence of his youth and was the beginning of his downhill slide. At fourteen, his parents were divorced, and at sixteen, his stepfather tossed him out of the house.

We would get high together and involve ourselves in all sorts of other nefarious activities. My father taught me how to deal and smuggle drugs and to be a gangster. This education drove me out on a limb and it was only a matter of time before it would break. At twenty-three, the branch broke, I had a drug overdose, which left me practically brain dead. I couldn't put two sentences together contiguously without losing my train of thought.

I sort of believed there was a higher power before I converted forty-four years ago. I knew Jesus walked the Earth as a historical figure, but I never understood that I could have a personal relationship with God, that God's love, joy, peace, patience, kindness, goodness, gentleness, faithfulness, and self-control could be mine.

Since giving my life to Christ, he has restored my mind, heart, soul, and body. Although some might argue to the contrary. God said to me, 'If you take care of my business (meaning, to live for Christ and proclaim his word), I will take care of yours,' and his miracle provision has never let me down. I realized that my tragedy was used by God to get my attention.

I have experienced the truth of his word in Romans 4:17b NASB, 'Even God who gives life to the dead and calls that which does not exist.' I realized that God is supernatural. He is always looking to take his super and make it natural in our lives. Jesus's love is eternal; his love never changes. My spiritual father, Pastor Jack, told me that it takes God's presence to work his purposes in our lives. God is just standing and waiting to penetrate our lives with his power and start working on our behalf.

God as the Trinity means that Jesus always was in heaven with the Father and the Holy Spirit. The way I understand the Trinity and the eternal nature of God is: the Father wills all life, the Son's word speaks all life, and the Holy Spirit does the work of accomplishing all life. The Trinity can be simplistically illustrated as a pencil. [A pencil] is one unit. However, it has three separate parts: the point, shaft, and eraser, and they have three distinct functions, yet, they are one indivisible item. Without one of those facets, you don't have a functioning pencil. This is how the Father, Son, and Holy Spirit work. It's an extraordinary expression of unity.

For anyone unfamiliar with Jesus, read the New Testament. The Bible is nothing more than the Manufacturer's handbook. When we read the Bible with faith, we learn about his love, and how to live as expressions of that love. For anyone who has never encountered Jesus, I suggest also reading C.S. Lewis's Mere Christianity and specifically the Book of John, the fourth book in the New Testament, and Josh McDowell's book More Than A Carpenter.

Josh McDowell is an elder Christian statesman, scholar, apologist, and personal friend. He goes into detail regarding the validity of scripture in his book and says that history is a knowledge of the past based upon testimony. So, for example, none of us were alive during the days of Napoleon, yet we believe in him historically because of the men and women who wrote about him and whom we have judged as being authentic.

Josh goes on to say that more than twenty thousand copies of the New Testament manuscripts are in existence as of 2009. The Iliad, second to the New Testament in manuscript authority, has only six hundred and forty-three manuscripts in existence. Craig Blomberg, former senior research fellow at Cambridge University in England and now professor of New Testament at Denver Seminary, explains that the texts of the New Testament have been preserved in far greater number and with much more care than any other ancient documents. He also concludes that ninety-seven to ninety-nine percent can be reconstructed beyond any reasonable doubt. So, there must be truth in all this.

Action Plan and Lesson

I know there are many of you who do not practice Christianity or who weren't brought up in a Christian household. That is okay. Needless to say, Christianity is the most popular religion in the world with over 2 billion followers. There must be something special about the Lord.

From my experience and PR's, we just want to encourage you to at least be open to try something new because we know that Jesus and God will never leave you or forsake you. You never know unless you try, so pick up the Bible, download the free YouVersion App, and start reading scripture. I read Scripture daily with the help of *Jesus Calling: Enjoying Peace in His Presence* by Sarah Young. Jesus's story in the Bible will illustrate God's love and inspire you to know you are not alone.

The Bible can help you find faith, transform your heart, and give you a fresh perspective. It will remind you that the hurdles in your life will be over sooner than you could imagine. It is a book of examples we can learn from as we watch ordinary people become extraordinary. Jesus and God might sound foreign for some to believe, but with these real experiences, it is my sincere desire to give you a greater sense of hope. For example, "Faith can move mountains" is from Matthew 17:20 and "Do everything in love" is from 1 Corinthians 16:14. They are synonymous and can be universally acknowledged. Anyone from any religion can say similar phrases.

Jeremiah 29:11 is one of my favorite verses in the Bible:

"For I know the plans I have for you," declares the Lord, "plans to prosper you and not to harm you, plans to give you hope and a future."

Whatever I am doing, I always remind myself of this verse.

With that, please try to place your trust in the hands of God or some higher power. When you have nothing else left in you, it is time to believe in something or someone greater than your control. Open your heart to hear God speak. He is always trying to reveal himself. He can do it simply through the words or actions of a stranger you meet on the street, or close personal friends and family. A chance encounter can change our lives forever. God is always working through others, like me, to help you heal and persevere. That is something beautiful to remember.

Whenever you lose faith, remember the words Jesus gave me, "Do not worry, everything is going to be okay," to fuel your soul.

Reflect

What or who is your source of faith?

What are some of your favorite faith-filled quotes?

Chapter 11

Integrate Your Intuition

Listen to your intuition. It will tell you everything you need to know.

—ANTHONY J. D'ANGELO

Sometimes the best decisions we make in life are the result of listening to our intuition. Our innate knowledge naturally exists within us just like gluten in wheat. Bread needs this protein to help it bind and rise when baking just like we need our intuition to help influence us to persevere.

There were many times my intuition kept telling me that I was on the right path and that everything, even cancer, was supposed to happen in my life.

I started to experience these feelings during the first week of 2017. I told my friend Alyssa that I had a gut feeling something major in my life was going to happen that year. I did not know what, but I knew my life was going to change.

Then something happened. A few months later, in March, I felt a lump the size of a golf ball on my neck during class. It came out of nowhere. I was quite worried, and immediately I had a bad feeling about it. My first instinct was that I was sick. I turned to my friend in class and said, "What is this? Do you think this is cancer?" And, at that moment, I foreshadowed a new and unexpected reality.

Because of my concern, I went to several doctors, had blood work done, and both an MRI and fine-needle biopsy. All the results were inconclusive and negative.

I let it go and continued to move on with my life. But I then started to encounter strange omens.

- Multiple days I kept seeing excessive pennies all over the floor, on my chair, and in my bed. I felt as if they were following me, and I was doing nothing to cause it.
- Twice I took my hand out of my pocket to find ladybugs hanging onto me for dear life, and when I tried to gently take them both off, they did not come off.

· The week before I was supposed to visit my last and final ENT specialist, butterflies kept swarming themselves around me, and in the most unusual places like the beach.

Because I had never experienced anything like this before, I researched the meaning behind these encounters. I found that these were all indicators from someone who had passed trying to talk to me. The only person I could think of was my grandfather, and after rationalizing with this, my inner voice told me that something was wrong with me.

All of these signs reappeared within the week I was scheduled to visit Dr. Godin for a second opinion on what the lump in my neck was caused by. I told my friend Alyssa that I knew my life was going to change in a week, and a few days later everything that I had a feeling about was confirmed. My life did change and I was diagnosed with cancer.

The second most profound time I experienced something like this was before I decided to write this book. Like I mentioned in the previous chapters, I was scared to open up about my cancer experience, so writing a book with raw and real stories from my experience seemed daunting to me. One night I had a dream that I was speaking on a stage in front of an audience, talking about my journey. When I woke up, I fought with it.

A few hours later, I saw the numbers 777 written on the bathroom's foggy mirror as I came out of the shower. I thought that was a little eerie, but I was also comforted because I knew this sign. I immediately looked up the meaning behind this number and discovered that it was my guardian angel telling me that I was heading in the right direction and that I needed to trust that I can bring light to the world. This later allowed me to focus on my intuition more to pursue the things I continued to dream of, which ultimately helped me catapult into my new chapter in life.

Story Time

Amanda Ianiri changed her life through the power of integrating her intuition to home in on her health-related issues. She did not see any signs from the universe, but she felt them in her gut. She tweaked her diet, turned around her mindset, and engaged in a community to uplift her and make her persevere.

It all started in my teens. I did not feel like a normal four-teen-year-old. I had unexplainable pelvic pain, was constantly going to doctors and the emergency room. I was in the hospital at least three times a month, and nobody could figure out what was wrong with me, even after MRIs, CT scans, and X-rays.

It got to the point where I was missing school, vomiting from the pain, and nothing would help me. One minute I was completely fine, running around on the playground, and then the next minute I am doubled over in pain, bawling my eyes out. Nobody understood. I was told it was in my head—that I was 'crazy.'

She knew something was wrong and was not convinced by what her health care providers were telling her. Two years later, Amanda discovered that the pain she was experiencing was endometriosis, an incurable condition that causes chronic inflammation due to tissue growth outside of the uterus, affecting 176 million women in the world, and was then hit with another diagnosis: she was diagnosed with polycystic ovary syndrome (PCOS).

To combat her unbearable pain, her doctors prescribed thirty different medications and birth control pills over the course of her treatment, but nothing was working. She felt defeated but had a feeling that she needed to keep finding alternative ways of coping.

I went from feeling on top of the world to feeling helpless. When you are told at the age of sixteen that you are going to have a disease for the rest of your life that causes chronic pain and infertility, you feel like you have no purpose. I was basing my life around my pain. I knew that I couldn't live with this for the rest of my life. This is when I decided I needed to make a change. I tried a holistic approach. I stopped all pharmaceutical treatment, and within two weeks I was a completely different person. I was more clear-headed, I was not as depressed, my pain was a lot better. It worked for me and changed the way I look at things.

I went on an anti-inflammatory diet and went plant-based. I could finally function normally. I was not going to the hospital anymore. Within a year, I only went to the hospital once instead of four times a month.

Just as she started to feel better, she moved to a different country, leaving her isolated and stressed. Amanda's symptoms unfortunately started to flare up again. This was when she knew that she needed to continue to take matters into her own hands and do more research on combating her limitations. One of her best remedies was finding a community of young women who were also experiencing her symptoms. She found support from online groups on Facebook that uplifted her and gave her hope.

These groups saved me. They were my outlet to make me feel understood. One thing that I struggled with was feeling so alone. I was not being heard at home because nobody understood what I was going through.

I got an overwhelming amount of support from women on social media. They were being so encouraging and understanding. Many would say things like, 'If you need anything, here is my number and email; send me a message.'" I even met someone who lives ten minutes away from me, which was comforting.

During this time, I also discovered a BuzzFeed video from a woman named Lara. She recorded a 'day in my life' video about living with endometriosis. I saw it and burst into tears because I related to it too much.

Finding support through these communities propelled me into finding purpose by helping others. My intuition told me to study biomedicine and nutrition, specialize in hormone therapy, and open up about my story to help others. I always knew at a young age I wanted to be my own boss, work for myself, and help society, but never knew what to do or how. My diagnosis propelled me to live with purpose. After everything, I realized that the one thing that made me feel good was bringing joy to others by helping them. I thought, 'If I can make a small impact on somebody's life to where they don't feel so alone, that's my goal.'

I had a lot of family members who did not agree with my career choice and way of healing, but my intuition and gut made me not care and want them [my career and healing] even more. I am so focused on trying to put my story out there to help other people and have already seen success because of the women who also have endometriosis I keep meeting through my journey. Because I have found successful ways to heal, I am helping them as well and plan on starting a YouTube channel.

I think every single thing that happens in life, happens for a reason, and I think that the reason why I got endometriosis was so that I could share my story with other people and uplift people and bring positivity and make them feel like they are not alone. I know this is my purpose, and I feel very aligned with my goals.

Action Plan and Lesson
Intuition comes into our lives during unique and troubling moments. It is essentially that "gut feeling" you may have that tells us, "Bubble in choice A instead of C" on a multiple-choice exam or to not eat that mystery

meat at the hot food bar. Interestingly enough, it all starts in the gut.

The gut's brain, so to speak, is known as the *enteric nervous system* (ENS). It consists of two thin layers of more than 100 million nerve cells lining your gastrointestinal system (esophagus to rectum), which sends signals to the central nervous system (CNS). The feelings you have in your gut reveals conscious thoughts. According to Jay Pasricha, director of the Johns Hopkins Center for Neurogastroenterology, "Our two brains [located in the gut and the skull] 'talk' to each other. This involves interactions between nerve signals, gut hormones, and microbiota—the bacteria that live in the digestive system."

Sometimes people do not know how to listen to their intuition or any signs that are leading them down the right path. Benson Simmonds, the energy healer, spiritual life coach, and author of *Soular Power,* says that you can connect with your instincts by tuning in, slowing down, and turning your dial inward. He says that "You just have to allow yourself to be and go. Intuition is underneath all senses; you see and feel it." This is similar to meditation, which I go more into detail about in the next chapter.

Benson says that the way to integrate your intuition is by grounding your feet on the floor and imagining divine light of unconditional love from the top of your head dissolving into your brain and heart. There is an internal resonance that will help you receive any messages from your higher-self.

First step is to turn off the external media, and tap into internal media (what is going on inside). It can be scary, of course, because you hear emotions, like fears and anxiety, and do not want to connect to them. You have to slow your body rhythm down and let go of your ego, which drives fear, lack, and limitation. You can eliminate the negative and download the positive. You just have to allow yourself to receive the light and let it flow; it changes everything.

The image I use with clients is a pie. When you are concerned with or anxious about something, your whole pie is absorbed with that problem. If you allow more light in, and slow down your body rhythm, the pie fills up with that and the thing you are anxious about gets smaller relative to the size of the pie.

We need to be careful about what we let influence our thoughts. If your inner self is trying to direct you on a path of healing, practice Benson's exercise and see if you can attend to any internal messages. That little voice inside of you is always trying to lead you down the right path. Even Abraham, a Source energy that is channeled through the famous spiritual coach Esther Hicks, says that intuition is our inner guidance:

Your inner being who can see way down the road who understands everything about everything, about everything that you want and need. If that thought came from there, it's not going to be a dud, it's not going to be a mistake.

With that, I encourage you to get in touch with your thoughts and see where they are leading you. Maybe you keep having "gut feelings," are seeing repeating "angel" numbers like 1111 or 444, or are constantly seeing phrases like "Everything is going to be okay." Remember that these are messages to help guide and comfort you so you can persevere on the right path. Recognize these signs and take note of them. It is essentially the universe trying to communicate with you, and if you have a feeling that they are leading you in the right direction, that is most likely the truth.

Reflect
What is your intuition telling you to do?

Chapter 12

Meditation is the Medication

The greater the difficulty, the greater the glory.

—MARCUS TULLIUS CICERO

Sometimes, the most difficult and time consuming practices are the best ones for your well-being. Like getting yourself to fall asleep at 10 p.m. instead of 1 a.m. to assure you get an adequate amount of sleep to help you feel energized, or forcing yourself to drink 72 oz. of water each day to hydrate and detox your body. What we need to realize is that the efforts we make to form a habitual routine will ultimately help us persevere. It is not impossible, but it takes an average of sixty-six days to form an automatic habit according to *Making Habits, Breaking Habits*. So, if you are really adamant about making a change, you need to be serious and dedicate yourself to your new routine.

One of the greatest habits that I engaged in was meditation. Any time I start to feel stressed, I automatically start to tune into my train of thought. I never truly understood how important mindfulness and meditation helps remedy negative thoughts until I tried it myself. As discussed in the last chapter, meditation helps you tune in to receive messages from the higher self to help guide you through your walk through life.

Meditation isn't about becoming a different person, a new person, or even a better person. It's about training in awareness and getting a healthy sense of perspective. You're not trying to turn off your thoughts or feelings. You're learning to observe them without judgment. And eventually, you may start to better understand them as well.

— Headspace Inc.

I discovered meditation one summer afternoon, just one month after my PowerPort was taken out of my chest. I was introduced to the solution of my discomfort by my friend and art gallery owner Georges Bergés. Although left with a scar across the top left side of my chest, I was trying to reclaim my body as the final memory of cancer was finally taken out of me. I was still unsure of who I was meant to be in this world. I did not feel comfortable in my own skin quite yet.

I was showing Georges some of the paintings I made during this troubling time. He identified that my distress was manifesting in my art—something that did not happen before. I did not realize it until he pointed it out and was rather surprised. I asked him, "How do you find yourself?" He responded, "You need to listen to your heart. You need to meditate." Based on his expertise, I trusted his word. This was the first time I took meditation seriously and gave it a try.

When I got home that day, I started to look up meditation guides on YouTube and began my practice. It took a few weeks to fully get the grasp of it. In fact, I was frustrated because of how difficult it was for me to sit or lie still. After some time, I was able to find my center and let my heart center speak to me. I started to become more comfortable with myself, my body, my being, and my purpose.

Amit Ray, a master of meditation, spiritual practice, and yoga, says, "Suffering is due to our disconnection with the inner soul. Meditation is establishing that connection." Thus, when one meditates, they free themselves of any despair. They become more mindful of their surroundings and body.

Meditation is our pathway to calmness. It is essentially a mental exercise that exhibits a mind-body connection. It helps people cope with their circumstances and brings calmness. MGH Psychiatric Neuroimaging Research Program's senior author, Sara Lazar, says that meditation "provides cognitive and psychological benefits that persist throughout the day," which proves that the neuroplastic changes, or the way the brain reorganizes neural connections, are a result of meditation.

These neuroplastic changes were discovered through a test by Benjamin Shapero, a scientific review officer for the Mechanisms of Emotion, Stress, and Health at Harvard Medical School, and Gaëlle Desbordes, a neuroscientist at Massachusetts General Hospital's Martinos Center for Biomedical Imaging. They conducted neuroimaging studies through the use of functional MRI (fMRI) tests. They discovered that after eight weeks, the control group training in meditation showed significant changes in the amygdala, the part of the brain that is the center for emotions and behavior. It was less activated after the meditation training.

Still not sold? The Center for Anxiety and Traumatic Stress Disorders at Massachusetts General Hospital conducted a randomized study on their patients and found that their Mindfulness-Based Stress Reduction (MBSR) program helped those who had generalized anxiety disorder (GAD). Their stress and coping mechanisms improved with the help of having a sense of mindfulness through meditation.

Story Time

I want to share with you how meditation helped a young female named Lana get out of drug addiction while she was in rehab, which ultimately inspired her to set her life back on a path where she has been led to help heal others.

Lana's story begins at the age of fourteen, when she first discovered cigarettes. She realized that she started to turn toward substance abuse because she did not fit into her own skin.

I was very anxious and sad. I went to school feeling like I wanted to throw up. My family dynamic was off, and I did not know how to cope. I loved the feeling of just kind of checking out, not feeling in my own skin. In high school, I just remember the thrill was more appealing to me. I never thought I could die from this. It was self-medicating.

[Drug use] started when I was sixteen, and when I was eighteen, it progressed. I tried heroin with a friend; 'We will snort it and not inject it,' she said. It seemed harmless and did not seem as bad [as injecting it with a needle].

This then led to painkillers, cocaine, and ecstasy. I said I was going to just use it on weekends when partying, then I started to use it after I finished exams, and it got out of control very quickly after a couple of months. It became an everyday activity. It was a daily habit.

When I was not using drugs, I was stuck. It felt like I needed to use it like a job I was getting paid for, and the scary part is that when I used the drugs, I did not get high anymore. I just felt normal, or sick. I was going through withdrawal and detoxing and felt like I was dying. My bones hurt everywhere, and I felt completely emotionally insane and suicidal. It was like the flu plus an emotional breakdown.

I remember sitting through lectures [in college], crying, and saying 'I can't do this anymore.' It got scary when I wanted to quit, but I couldn't. [Stopping the usage] kept getting pushed back. I went home one weekend and told myself that I was

not going to get high, and the next thing you know, I was
blacked out on autopilot.

I noticed bad habits, like lying, cheating, and stealing, were
coming along with using drugs. It was terrible. It was very
clear to me that I couldn't live with drugs. I just had terrible
ideas of the world and myself.

Lana finally started to center herself, listen to her
intuition, and try to find the help she knew she needed.
During her freshman year of college, she went to out-
patient therapy after she continued to have episodes
of blacking out, being unconscious, and waking up in
a wet bed.

At first, [therapy] was tough because I kept arguing that I
wanted to keep smoking and drinking like a normal eighteen-
year-old girl even if those two things were not me 'things'
(as were hard drugs). So, I did. I told my counselor I was not
going to do heroin and cocaine when [smoking and drinking],
but then every time I would. I went right back to harder
drugs without fail, like clockwork.

At the time all of this was going on, someone at my high
school had died of an overdose. We had the same dealer
and picked up [the use of drugs] at the same time. Then I

remember saying to myself, 'Wow, that could have been me,'
and then hoped it was.

I knew I needed more intensive treatment, and my therapist
recommended an inpatient program where I would live at
a halfway house in Florida for thirty days. In rehab, I just
remember feeling like so relieved for the first time that I was
in the care of other people like me.

I did not want to ruin my life; I wanted to be clean. [Getting
high] was not fun, it was an illusion of fun, it was misery. I
was scared of not having this 'normal college life.' And, you
know, luckily, in a group therapy session, people talked me
into staying in treatment and getting help.

There were moments of doubt or thinking it was not going
to work out. It was fear of the unknown, but one of the steps
in the program was turning over your will to a higher power
of your understanding through meditation.

Meditation was one of the best things that happened
to Lana. She learned to be patient and was able to find
peace and security in herself, something that she never
thought was possible before. She learned how to meditate for the first time at a class in a nondenominational
chapel. During this time, she remembers lying down

on a pew and experiencing a sense of satisfaction with who she was, even in her situation.

I remember saying, 'Everything is okay because I am on my own path.' I had hope that I could be restored to sanity and feel like a whole person. This was the first moment of relief.

[The meditation leader] reassured the class that it will be hard to find peace in the beginning, especially right after becoming sober because the brain is rewiring itself. She encouraged the class to accept and embrace the small moments. She said that even if it was a moment that lasted only five seconds, letting your head be still will help you have longer periods of peace and serenity through continued mindfulness practice.

When I returned home after a month, I was isolated and angry. I got through it by becoming my own best friend. I just liked to enjoy my own time and be okay with the fact that it was a Saturday night and I was by myself while everybody was out partying. I was doing my own thing and was comfortable in my own company, which was so valuable.

I knew [recovery] was about transformation. My father texted me: 'There is no growth in comfort, and no comfort in growth.'

The biggest internal transformation was going on inside of me [because of meditation], and gradually an emotional maturity grew too. I was taught how to be a person again. I was the happiest I'd ever been. I felt understood, like I wasn't alone. I saw how that time [in Florida] served me so well. I knew my best years were ahead of me.

Most people want a quick fix, but it is tedious and difficult work. [The work] is uncomfortable, but healing. One of the things we say in the program is 'The therapeutic value of one addict helping another is without parallel.' I'm firm believer that people who have similar experiences are so crucial in helping you get through the bad stuff.

Lana continued to listen to that little voice inside her head, continued to center herself, and stayed on the road she dreamed of: sobriety. She attended meetings with Narcotics Anonymous, a support group that aided her recovery process and acted as a source of therapy, and with a hospitals and institutions (H&I) subgroup that goes to hospitals, institutions, and neighboring sites to bring awareness to the benefits and hope in recovery. She was also invited to participate in Harmonium, a nonprofit organization that provides support to clean and sober people at festivals, at a three-day music festival called Governors Ball.

Lana has now been able to take her healing to another level and help others in detox centers, psychiatric wards, and prisons. She says that telling these people about the programs she was in is rewarding because she knows how they feel and knows that reassuring them of recovery is possible.

There was this one man who came to me and said 'You were at my detox when you were a very young person, and wow, now you are here!' I learned that the best thing you can give someone is an ear because [someone else's] pain is important and relevant.

Action Plan and Lesson

It is quite amazing how Lana used the power of her thoughts to transform her mind. She was able to free herself from her pain through her community. This inspired her to take her gift of healing to a new level. She used this practice as a tool to find her true calling and has been able to live it out to this day. Lana is a practicing acupuncturist, but she would have never found such purpose and passion in such an intimate healing process if it was not for her experience through meditation.

Just like Lana, you can engage in meditation to help you find peace with your struggle. A good way to begin your meditation is through breathwork.

Dr. Joshua Kantor, a chiropractor and kinesiologist, I worked with, helped me center myself through this practice. He taught me to follow a 4-7-8 rule. Breathe in for 4 seconds, hold for 7, release for 8. I use this to quiet my mind and body. The increased flow of oxygen helps in supporting the body's central nervous system to calm down. I also enjoy breathing exercises Gabrielle Bernstein discusses in *Judgment Detox: Release the Beliefs That Hold You Back from Living A Better Life*.

Another way you can meditate is by engaging in gratitude and mindfulness. Dr. Josh Axe, a doctor of natural medicine, says that he does a spiritual triathlon every morning to fulfill these two practices. The first five minutes he spends praising God and looking at his vision board, then he reads the Bible or a personal growth book, and finally sits in visualization.

When engaging in any of these meditative practices, the one tip I would suggest is to not get discouraged. There are so many different types of meditation that you can engage in.

Here are a few:

- Metta
- Body scanning
- Transcendental
- Spiritual
- Movement
- Guided
- Breath
- Mantra

I believe you will be able to find a way to center yourself, and meditation is a great way to start. I would suggest using one as a starting point. My favorite is guided meditation, but sometimes I like to play Solfeggio frequencies while engaging in breath work. These are an ancient collection of musical scales that were used in singing and chanting using different soundwave frequencies. Today, they are a form of sound therapy and play a specific role in helping tuning into our higher self, releasing fears, healing relationships, repairing DNA, and more.

Reflect
How will you engage in meditation?

Chapter 13

Expressing Yourself through Art

Don't ask yourself what the world needs; ask yourself what makes you come alive. And then go and do that. Because what the world needs is people who have come alive.

—*HOWARD THURMAN*

Do you find that you tend to turn toward activities that you enjoyed as a child? Instead of dancing in a ballet, maybe you attend a performance in a theater, and instead of playing on a tennis team, maybe you take your rackets out on the weekend and play a casual match with friends, or perhaps you take your passion to a new level and pursue it as a career. Either way, these interests and likes trigger internal fireworks. This light helps us persevere

During treatment, I asked one of my infusion nurses if she could suggest something to me to help me mentally cope with everything I was experiencing. Although I am grateful for the life lessons cancer has taught me, I am also human. I have my moments like everyone, and feeling my body deteriorate was very hard for me to undergo, both physically and mentally.

I knew I needed to find a coping mechanism to release my emotions. It was suggested by my healthcare practitioners that I tap into my childhood hobbies and embrace them. I was always drawn to using creative outlets to center myself from a young age, so I pursued art as my coping mechanism.

After arriving home from the infusion center, I immediately brought my stepstool to my bedroom, opened my closet, reached for the box of paint, my collection of brushes, and a small 8"x 24" blank canvas, and took them to my desk. I left them out to use the following day.

The next morning, I anxiously stared at my supplies. I did not know what to do with them. It had been so long since I created art in general that I felt semi-paralyzed. Despite my hesitation, I assembled my workspace, dipped my brush into gold paint, and started to make strokes onto the blank canvas. There was no objective or theme in my abstract piece, but the way my brush hit the canvas was so therapeutic to me. I was expressing myself through the practice of painting.

At the end of my painting session, I was able to release anger and frustration. I ultimately felt at peace. It was like my meditation, although I used more meditation to tap into my manifested emotions on canvas as discussed in the last chapter. I was able to forget about the world around me and home into my true nature through art. I was engaging in an activity that made me feel at home with myself. I was born an artist and finally was able to use art as a way to express what I was unable to articulate in words. I continued to paint every week. One thing lead to another, and something extraordinary occurred.

People started to recognize my passion and order paintings to collect in their homes. Now, I am a commissioned painter. How crazy is that?

Aside from my endeavor, I believe that everyone is an artist at heart. Pablo Picasso once said, "Art washes from the soul the dust of everyday life," and I truly believe so. The world is full of creativity. From the architectural details in our homes, to the colors in our wardrobe and the shapes of the magnets on our refrigerator doors, we are constantly surrounded by artistic imagination. It fuels us, defines us, and is in particular meant to heal. It has been proven to help people formulate their emotions to create change.

Story Time

Art therapist, Janina Diaz-Solari, says that art is one of the main tools she has found to identify any subconscious disturbances in her personal and professional life. When her friend passed away from a sudden cancer diagnosis, Janina was devastated. She was inspired by Frida Kahlo, a Mexican artist who used art as a way to express her aggression and chronic pain, and turned toward art as a healing mechanism to deal with her psyche.

I saw the power in that, and I started [to paint like Frida as well]. Then, I came across an art therapist that came to a museum I worked in who told me about art therapy, how it is the combination of art and psychology. I loved the sound of it, and I decided that was something that I want to pursue. I now felt a sense of satisfaction and purpose.

Early in her career, Janina worked with pediatric patients in the oncology department at Mount Sinai Hospital and New York University to help normalize their environment through artistic means. She connected their psyche with art to help them cope with whatever they were going through. Her main goal was to make it as much about helping the patients remember what their coping skills were to take on the challenge of dealing with their pain, and art happened to be one of the least costly ones.

One of the most successful forms was through mandala making. This practice involves creating wholeness in geometrical circular structures with different shapes and patterns that symbolize our infinite being.

Pema Chödrön, an American Tibetan Buddhist, says that "each person's life is like a mandala—a vast, limitless circle. We stand in the center of our own circle, and everything we see, hear, and think forms the mandala of our life." Mandalas overall represent self-unity and peace. The circles of the mandala represent sacred space and can be symbols of intention.

I tell my clients to actually visualize the pain or whatever the anger is, inside the mandala with a certain color, and then tell them to create another mandala with opposite colors. Colors equate emotions, and this exercise helps with that. If you're thinking of sadness, then you have to think of the opposite, which is happiness. If you're thinking of anxiety, then think of being anxiety free. This is dialectical behavioral therapy (DBT).

This way of addressing the mandala helps you to create a place where things inspire you. Creating a sense of safety and a soothing quality while you are making them gives you a higher sense of yourself. You feel a relaxing calmness throughout the whole mandala-making session. It makes my patients feel better, even with those who are detoxing from substance abuse. The repetitive nature makes you feel comfortable. It's self-soothing.

There were three cases that were assigned to Janina that dealt with bone marrow transfers, which were in special sterile centers. She was unable to bring supplies to the unit because of the risk of contaminating the patients with bacteria and germs, so she practiced a different form of art: visualization. She would use colors in meditation to help them feel less pain. So instead of seeing red, she would help the patients see white, similar to what Benson said in Chapter 11. This helped with pain management.

I would have the patients think of a color within a circle, and the pain would be transferred in the intensity of the color. I would have them reduce the intensity by turning that circle into a white circle. It focused them into making that change in the color, like Ericksonian Hypnosis from the psychiatrist and psychologist Dr. Milton Erickson, who specialized in neurolinguistic programming.

The white color was a way be pain free. A lot of patients saw red. The intensity of the red would be the intensity of the pain, and white would act as lacking pain, or freedom from it.

A lot of my adult patients are hesitant with art. Whether it is through visualization or in tangible form, once you become aware of yourself as an artist, you can address a lot of issues in your art where it does not get addressed verbally. Art really brings up a lot of unconscious material. It gives them hope that they can heal.

Action Plan and Lesson

Overall, art has proven to show significant improvement in the psyche. It helps people express things that are too difficult to put into words and gives them an outlet to reduce stress. Art therapy has been clinically proven to help patients cope. A study done through Chelsea and Westminster Hospital, Staricoff found that groups that engaged in creative work had "better vital signs, diminished cortisol related to stress, and less medication needed to induce sleep." Another study done by Heather L. Stuckey, DEd and Jeremy Nobel, MD, MPH concluded the following:

- Creative expression is linked to emotional healing and greater wellness.
- Artistic self-expression helps form a positive self-identity.
- Art can help *replace difficult* verbal expression.
- Guided imagery helps relieve pain by focusing on positive life experiences.

Whether you are creating mentally or tangibly, any form of creative artistry helps place the psyche from one mindset to another. Painting helped me heal, which ultimately allowed me to persevere. Having the freedom to choose which colors I wanted to paint with helped me create a story of my emotions on canvas, which ultimately made me feel like I was in control of my circumstances. For example, red could have helped me identify that I was subconsciously angry, and blue could have suggested that I was calm.

Because art has such great benefits? I would suggest buying either a mandala-making book from your local bookstore and colored pencils or pens, or canvas, paint, and brushes. Pay attention to the colors you choose because this can reveal more on your mood and thoughts. Through art, we can become our own healers.

Reflect

What color do you categorize your pain to be in, and how does this manifest in your day-to-day life?

What creative outlet do you turn to when coping with a struggle?

Chapter 14

Fueling Up

Let food be thy medicine and medicine be thy food.

—HIPPOCRATES

I hope that you were inspired to explore meditation and art and reflect on how they have helped fuel your mental health. There are more activities that you can engage in to help further your progression in overcoming your trials. I want to fuel your confidence and well-being with a story from Nicole Foster, a courageous, dear friend of mine who I was introduced to through mutual friends from college while I was going through treatment. She was my backbone during my darkest days because she experienced very similar emotions. Nicole is the perfect example of someone who was able to find success in many of the previous topics I discussed, and more. The one thing that played a key role in her perseverance was the power of food.

What you eat affects the way you show up on a day-to-day basis. Whatever you digest turns into energy for your body to use. Food is supposed to nourish you, and when your gut is not absorbing the right nutrients, you will not be able to perform and function at your greatest potential.

Finding a balance with food was something I battled with during my cancer journey. During treatment I lost all sense of taste and the foods I used to enjoy, and I was unable to eat any raw vegetables and fruits, foods that I usually opted for to give me energy. Everything made me nauseous, and between the bottles of steroids I had taken on a daily basis and my infusion cocktail, my gut biome was imbalanced and my body was unable to absorb the nutrients it needed.

It was not until I ended all treatment that I was able to reclaim my health and vitality through the foods I ate. I started to work with a functional nutritionist who tested my food sensitivities, intolerances, and levels of inflammation, and developed a protocol specifically tailored to my body to help me heal. In just one month, I felt improvements in my energy and mood. I was a completely different person because of how I was nourishing my body from the inside. Food is helping me persevere everyday and can help you too.

Story Time

Nicole has gone through a series of unfortunate childhood traumas. She describes her life as "unconventional" because she had to mature at a rate much different from her friends. When she was of the age of five, she lost her father to the September 11th terrorist attacks on the Twin Towers, and the age of fourteen, she was diagnosed with cancer.

During these two vulnerable times in her life, Nicole was able to recognize one main theme: kindness. People went out of their way to be sympathetic and show their affection to help Nicole during her troubling times. After experiencing this, she knew she was destined to give back to others. Her unexpected cancer experience is what ultimately influenced her to see the importance of giving back to her community.

I was on a walk with my friends along the beach on Fourth of July, and halfway through walking the boardwalk, I was in pain and felt exhausted. This was extremely unusual.

I called my mom to pick me up and thought it may just be a stomachache. I went home to rest. Two days after the patriotic holiday, I was still tired, exhausted, and gained unexplained bruises—this combination finally led us to the doctor. Those seemingly random symptoms pointed to bigger issues:

*my spleen was enlarged, and my white blood count was at
zero. I was directed to immediately go to Morristown Medical
Center Hospital in New Jersey.*

*I did not know what I was about to endure, or the technical-
ities of anything. I was diagnosed with acute promyelocytic
leukemia (APML), a type of blood cancer. I was hospitalized
for twenty-nine days. I did not understand the concept of
cancer and how sick I was at my young age. The doctors did
not know the cause as well. I was not sure if I was going to die.*

*I was on so many different steroids, including one to help
prevent my eyes from turning blue from the chemo and one
to treat an infected lymph node in my face. I was very worried. It was also a very vulnerable time because all of my hair
fell out in clumps at the hospital overnight.*

*It got very real during this time. It was intense. One of the
biggest things people told me was to stay strong, but it was
hard to hear that when I was going through the toughest
thing ever. Though, I realized I had to take on this challenge,
be courageous, and get through it.*

Interestingly enough, the three main activities that
helped Nicole persevere during this time have been
discussed in the previous chapters. Every single day,
she prayed the Angel of God Prayer:

Angel of God, my guardian dear,
to whom God's love commits me here,
ever this day be at my side,
to light and guard, to rule and guide.
Amen.

She read affirmations and positive quotes every day, such as "Courage does not always roar. Sometimes courage is the quiet voice at the end of the day saying, 'I will try again tomorrow.'" by Mary Anne Radmacher. And she kept herself busy through arts and crafts.

Once she recovered from what she described as a jarring hospital stint, she was back at school a few months later like every other sophomore, and finally, during her senior year, on January 29, 2014, she was able to say she was done with treatment.

I could not do much; I tried to find ways to be involved in things, but it was too hard. I could not go to prom or any major events. After high school, I moved on to college. People did not know I had cancer; I felt like cancer differentiated me whether they knew it or not. It was challenging. This was the hardest part. I could not relate to anyone."

This is when Nicole took the opportunity to start to focus on herself, to not allow the college culture to influence her in a negative way but empower her to change for the best. Her life transformed before her eyes. She used her memories in the hospital as a cancer patient to inspire her to take control of her diet with the help of a health and wellness coach and fellow survivor she found on Instagram. Through this, Nicole was able to find the strengths in diet, transition her daily intake of food, and reclaim her health and well-being.

Nicole began to eat real, nourishing, whole, plant-based foods and began to incorporate exercise, such as yoga and running, into her daily routine. She started to feel more alive and comfortable in her own skin. With her daily practices of prayer, creative engagement, and positive affirmations, adding this lifestyle change was the missing ingredient to the recipe. She was able to finally persevere. Because of this, she was inspired to use this fuel to help share her grace with others.

I was given the gift of survival, and two-years post-cancer treatment, I realized I wasn't living up to my potential. I lost sixty pounds, and my healthier diet made me more confident to go to the gym and be active. I realized that food affects your mood, so now I am more cautious about what I eat.

As Nicole started to feel healthier, she started to become more confident in helping others. Food was the reason

Nicole was able to persevere. Nicole started to open up about her experience and used her power to give back to her community in the most fulfilling way to allow other patients to see that there is hope on the other side.

I raised over $40,000 for The Valerie Fund and participated in their little survivor book called The Voices. This was the center where I was treated, and after feeling healthy again from my new lifestyle, I wanted to show other patients that there is hope on the other side. After, I heard from a high school friend that the young girl who she babysits who was recently diagnosed with cancer saw my photo in this book and told her mom, 'I am going to be a survivor just like her.' This was an incredibly humbling gift.

Nicole has also participated in many other initiatives like Foxes Fight Cancer and For the Record to raise cancer awareness and share her story on her college campus at Marist College. She has even gotten a certification through the Institute for Integrative Nutrition (IIN) and coaches clients through her platform @seededsoul on Instagram. These have enabled her to see the positive in all that she has gone through.

Choosing to live well does not mean perfectionism but finding balance and being more present and mindful. Cancer shaped me and my struggles and made me realize what is worth my

time and energy. I still have insecurities like everyone else,
but I know what I am capable of now. Because of the lifestyle
changes I have made, I am able to show up for others and
help them in ways that helped me before.

Action Plan and Lesson

The power of food helped Nicole thrive and spread a
message of kindness and compassion to others. She is
now able to show up in the world with confidence. From
her perspective, "being healthy" is choosing to truly
take care of and honor your body. It all comes down to
respecting bio-individuality. Biologist Eran Segal states
that we all have our own biological make-up and need to
have specific diet plans tailored for our unique bodies.
The way that we fuel up should be adjusted to our one-
of-a-kind lives, and that is pretty awesome.

Nonetheless, I can understand if you have a goal to lose a
set amount of weight in a short period of time, but what
if it does not happen? Are you going to beat yourself up
for getting distracted with other priorities? Sometimes
setting a time-framed goal will only put unhealthy and
stressful pressure on yourself because some goals are
impossible to achieve when you want them to be, and
it is okay.

In order to reap the benefits of food, it is important to become mindful of what you put in your body. Nicole says there is no perfect formula for improving your health, but there are some universally applicable tips that have made a big difference in her life. Here are a few of her suggestions:

- Eat whole foods such as fruits, vegetables, whole grains, and healthy fats.
- When buying produce, be mindful of the "Dirty Dozen" and choose organic foods to reduce pesticide exposure.
- Don't force yourself to eat foods you hate. Rather, prepare and nourish yourself with healthy foods that are enjoyable.
- Strive for progress, not perfection, and implement balance.
- Do not compare yourself to others. Instead, become inspired by the food choices you may see others make.
- Learn how to prepare simple and easy meals from a step-by-step blog post or video.
- Be aware that there is not a cure-all protocol for everyone, but do consider implementing superfoods into your diet because they are proven to be incredibly powerful and antioxidant-rich.

See? It is not too difficult to make healthier choices. Just remember that taking control of your well-being does not mean diving right into a juice cleanse or preparing to train for a triathlon. Rather, it can be as simple as choosing to take the time to make a smoothie with spinach, berries, and almond milk for breakfast or squeezing in a light walk after dinner to help you digest. Regardless of your limitations, there are ways to live well and improve your health and well-being.

Reflect

What lifestyle changes will you make to help fuel your day?

How will food help fuel you?

Chapter 15

Finding Community

Quality of life actually begins at home - it's in your street, around your community.

—*CHARLES KENNEDY*

I think we can all agree that when we find others who are in the same situation as us, we are able to feel less alone and more hope-filled. The feeling of comfort we receive from our communities allows us to become our own champions. Essentially, it is an essential element of humanity. From the days of the Paleolithic Era, to the Middle Ages and the Modern Era, humanity has thrived only off of companionship. We are a social species. It is ingrained in our blood.

Maintaining social environments has been scientifically proven to be essential in order to thrive. Let's look at the famous psychologist Abraham Maslow's theory of Hierarchy of Needs. His model states that the core of survival is sequenced in order from the most important to the least:

- Physiological needs—water, food, and shelter
- Safety needs—financial security and health
- Love and belonging—a sense of connection through friendships, family, and intimacy
- Esteem—respect, recognition, and status
- Self-actualization—desire to become our best self

The main point I want to focus on here is the third most important: love and belonging. This means that his research found that it is absolutely crucial to develop interpersonal relationships in order to survive. Without having a sense of support or affiliation, we will not be able to persevere. Communities allow us develop healthy ecosystems to aid in the feeling of belonging.

As you were able to read from many of the previous stories, having someone else to connect to helped most people thrive. Personally, having a sense of community is what helped me understand that there were others in a similar position as me. Whenever I felt hopeless, I would find comfort through online support groups and connect with individuals who had similar stories and symptoms. One of my most profound moments was when I connected with a group of five young ladies over brunch one Saturday afternoon who had all just overcome different types of blood cancer. When we all met, we were strangers, but after going around the table and sharing our stories, we all befriended each other. This was the first time I met survivors who were just like me. I felt a sense of normalcy.

Story Time

A similar situation happened to a young man named Andrew, who addressed his feeling of hopelessness by finding different communities he felt he belonged to. He started to realize he was different around the age of ten. Around that time, Andrew was diagnosed with two learning disabilities and suffered from a speech impediment. He always knew he was different from everyone around him, and that negatively affected him.

Once I found out that I had dyslexia and ADHD, I thought I was the defective individual in my family. It was me versus my brother, who was much smarter than me and always graduated with honors. I was a slow reader and [in school], I was constantly told by my teachers that I was not going to get into college or even graduate high school.

Andrew was bullied and harassed for being different. He could not keep up with his peers and decided to attend a school that specialized in disabilities for a few years.

Distraught and depleted, he lost his sense of worth because of the way others viewed him.

I was known as 'weird' and was not the greatest student [academically]. This affected my mental health and led me down dark paths. It took me longer to do schoolwork and other normal activities my peers were involved in, and I couldn't [mentally] handle it.

One night, I attempted suicide and got hospitalized for telling my friend how I felt unsafe. I was sent away to a therapeutic wilderness program in Hawaii called Pacific Quest for three months. There were no cell phones allowed. We all wore the same clothes, had matching sandals, slept in the same cabin, and farmed and produced our own food. Specifically, [farming my own food] made me realize that I can do anything myself. I made it myself and saw that I was able to do whatever I set my mind to.

During the program, I was able to see everyone was in the same boat as me. Watching my peers grow also helped me. I was with people who had a wide variety of disabilities and backgrounds like drug and physical abuse, PTSD, and drug overdose. When we applied ourselves and worked together during different activities, it was very eye-opening and beautiful. We had to break down the barrier of the law that defined us and that people in the past created for us.

We all went through different things, but felt exactly the same. It was not until we had a group therapy session and I heard everyone else's stories and started to cry for no reason that I saw that we all suffered. We had all of this anger, frustration, sadness, and despair and were dealing with the same emotions.

It was not until I saw others express [those feelings] that I was able to move forward and realize I did not have to have these emotions bottled up. I did not have to keep in what others [from my old schools] told me about myself. Instead, I could let it out and let myself decide. I learned that it is a growing and learning process.

After the program, I knew who I was; I was going to go out there and make a name for myself. I was not going to let people decide who I was, like all of those teachers who told me that I could not amount to something. I let them decide that for me, but I finally realized I can do whatever I set my mind to. I was my own individual, and no one can tell me that I cannot accomplish big things.

Andrew's sense of community propelled him into purpose. When he got back home, his parents sent him to a new school that specializes in accommodating children with learning disabilities. He was now going to be part of a community where he felt like he belonged. However, whenever he had fear of acclimating himself back into society, he was able to use a three-step routine he learned at Pacific Quest to get him out of his wariness. Andrew first broke apart the scene of negative experience, then understood why it was causing distress and affecting him, and once finding the reason, he finally took it out of his equation and incorporated activities he loved into his day-to-day routine. Whether it was participating in activities such as running, swimming, wrestling, or playing an instrument with others, he was more relaxed and hope-filled.

Engaging in a community where he felt accepted and loved paid off. He was able to successfully complete high school and got accepted into the most competitive college he applied to. When he went to college, he took the opportunity to continue to build a supportive network by joining ROTC and the crew team. At the end of Andrew's sophomore year, he decided to study psychology in special education for his undergraduate degree so he can be a companion for students similar to him. Now, Andrew is teaching in Fulbright's English Teaching Assistant (ETA) Program in Malaysia to help grow communities that help children in underdeveloped and low-income areas.

Andrew started to find his potential and accept all that he was born with and went through. The support he found through his community strengthened him with the gift of purpose. "Having a sense of purpose actually relates to living a longer, happier life. When we feel we are sharing our unique gifts with others, we feel useful, appreciated, validated, and meaningful," according to the physician Mark Hyman. Since finding these traits through a community can make you feel like you matter, it's worth branching out and finding your own community to bolster you.

We are all on a different path, and every experience we have in life is just a stone in that path. Where we place that stone decides where we are going to go. If you want to move forward [from something bad], you have to realize that it is just one negative factor in a larger scheme. You can move forward as long as you take it with a grain of salt and place that stone in an area where it will help move to a brighter future. It is not in the end of the world; it's not going to decide the next ten, twenty, or thirty years.

[Whatever hardship you are experiencing] will just hurt in the moment. Let the future come to you. If you have made it this far, keep going. Just look back at where you were, and now where you are. We can do phenomenal things; we just need the right motivation. We have all the potential.

Action Plan and Lesson

The resources available to Andrew were stepping stones that placed him on the path he was meant to walk. He is excelling beyond his wildest dreams and and is continuing to live a fruitful and passionate life. He knows that his community allowed him to persevere and continue to make a positive impact on the lives of others. Andrew used his greatest insecurity as his best asset and has not let his disabilities define him. Just like Mahatma Gandhi said, "Be the change that you wish to see in the world." When you live against the odds, you can impact many.

When you are searching for the right community for you, it might be intimidating at first. Once you acclimate, you will feel like you have a sense of purpose and belonging that can then escalate and help impact others. In order to find a community of your own, I would suggest starting local. Research programs that meet on a regular basis and see how you can get involved. If you are a regular at church, see if you can volunteer at your parish every weekend. If your true passion is creating awareness about our ecosystem and climate change, connect with bloggers online and attend coffee corner conversations on how to live sustainably. If seeking support in your regional area is difficult, find online comfort and start a conversation thread. You never know who you will meet and what lives you will impact. Whether it is virtual or in person, find your cause, sign up for the next meeting, and attend.

Reflect

What is one way you can impact your community?

Chapter 16

Be Patient with Your Time

The Universe is not trying to break you, my dear, it's trying to find a way to wake you up, so that you will see what is real, and worth fighting for. It takes time to heal, but it also takes courage.

—REBEKAH LETCH

Do you ever feel like time harbors impatience, especially when you are placed under pressure or desire to see immediate outcomes? Like the infamous example of an anxious child repetitively asking the bus driver, "Are we there yet?" every minute of the hour-drive to the amusement park. Nothing can change to make the distance from point a to b go faster. Okay, fine. If I must digress, you could essentially argue that the driver can arrive faster by speeding, but essentially the mileage is the same. Plus, trying to cheat your way out of the natural process of things can do more harm than good. This is why you must be patient with your time.

"Time" was *the* four letter word that I kept hearing after every conversation I had with my doctors, family members, and alternative healers. While I was receiving my last treatment, I realized that this was the last time I would be sitting through a four-hour infusion. My excitement was taking over, and I knew that this was my moment of freedom. When I asked my nurse when I was going to start to feel better, she responded with ambiguity.

Patients start to feel back to normal after three months, but I do not know. Everyone is different. You have to just give it time.

This seemed like an unbearable timeframe. Three more months? Yikes. I wanted to feel better right away.

The three months passed and to my surprise, I started to feel worse as my body was detoxing from the poison it had received for four months straight. There was nothing I could do to feel a sense of normalcy.

After I started school about nine months after cancer treatment was over, I still did not feel like the Alexa I use to know. I did not have enough energy to engage in the normal college social engagements I used to enjoy, like attending evening club meetings, watching late-night movies with roommates, and staying up until the wee hours of the night with classmates baking chocolate chip cookies to try to keep us up while studying for finals. My fatigue robbed me of enjoyment, and I started to put an unnecessary pressure on myself.

However, whenever I began to fall into the trap of self-comparison, I told myself that I needed to utilize my time more wisely. I made it a goal to spend every precious moment occupying myself with things that fulfilled me. I took the time to engage in different activities like yoga, afternoon tea dates with friends, and evening meditation. Months later, I reaped the benefits and started to feel more energized. This enabled me to soar. I was persevering in the way I thought was out of reach.

Another example is Matthew Zachary. He also understood the benefits of time. After he was diagnosed with pediatric brain cancer at the age of twenty-one, he utilized his time to create something he was passionate about. He started Stupid Cancer, a community where other young adults like him could express themselves. Today it is now the largest young adult cancer support group. Because of his experience and all that he went through, he has been able to inspire, impact, and provide emotional support to thousands of patients worldwide and has been featured in *Time* magazine and *The Washington Post* and on Fox News and MTV, to name a few. His negative experience allowed him to utilize his time to help others persevere in ways that the last chapter even discussed, and you have the ability to do the same.

Story Time

I want to share with you a story about how Isaiah Lamb, a former Division I basketball player, was able to trust the divine timing of his life. When Isaiah, who was born and raised in Baltimore, was young, his parents lost everything. From the time he was in seventh grade to his senior year in high school, he and his whole family were left homeless.

Their displacement started after Isaiah's father suffered a heart attack. He was unable to work as a maintenance man and found himself out of work, leaving the family's income dependent solely on his mother. It was tough for the family to sustain their living standards with one low-paying source of income.

As their finances started to decrease, they moved their belongings from one apartment to the next until eviction. After being thrown out of their living spaces, they rented a room at a motel. When their financial resources became depleted, their last resort was their Hyundai Elantra. For months, they spent their nights sleeping in the parking lot of a 24-hour coin laundromat.

I was in the back with clothes and my bookbag. It was very cramped, especially with me being six foot three. This was my normal way of life, and it was just overwhelming. I did not want people in the neighborhood to see me; we would always make sure no one was around the parking lots. I started to then live separately from my family and crashed at either a friend's or my coach's house.

Thankfully, in my senior year, my parents got a place to live near my high school. There was no furniture or anything. We just used it as shelter.

"'It does not last forever,'" my mom preached to me.

Isaiah used his time doing the things he loved and made a vision of the life he wanted to live in the future. Just as he was using sports as a distraction to get his mind off of what he was going through, Isaiah's life started to continue to spiral downhill. He tore one ACL in the ninth grade, losing a full scholarship to play for Rutgers University's football team, and then tore another in twelfth grade, losing ten out of his twelve Division I collegiate basketball offers. He spiraled into a deep depression because he thought he was never going to go to college, but then something happened.

Just as he thought his life was falling apart, his parents were able to save enough money to move into a small apartment in Baltimore his senior year. Shortly after, he received an unexpected phone call from a journalist from *Sports Illustrated* magazine. "We heard your story and want to interview you," Jon Wertheim said. This was a miracle, just in the nick of time.

I thought he was joking. I gave the phone to my mother, and she said that it was actually real. Jon wanted to come to Baltimore and interview us in person for the 'Young, Gifted and Homeless' segment. I still to this day do not know who contacted him because I never told anyone what I was going through.

When he came here, we took some photos. A few weeks later, he invited me and my dad to New York for the magazine release. He showed us the cover, and it was a photo of me! It was a surprise. Right after this, I was offered a full scholarship to Marist College to play on the Marist men's Division I basketball team. A big weight was lifted off my shoulders. My mother was right. Everything worked out in the time it was supposed to.

Action Plan and Lesson

In time and through hope, Isaiah's life turned around and opened before his eyes. Today, Isaiah has completed his undergraduate degree in business and has taken his basketball efforts as his professional career. He is now the owner of a fitness brand called Lo-Lamb Company and a personal trainer. He uses his athletic experience to help others take their fitness to the next level. Isaiah remained patient with the way his life was going to unfold, and he is now persevering.

Nothing lasts forever, even if it seems rough and there is no other way, it will not last for too much longer. Just have a positive mindset and keep pushing through. Things are tough and are not always going to be good, but you have to look at the good side of things and appreciate what you do have. [Everyone has] SOMETHING to be thankful for.

Remember, things happen on God's terms, not your terms. You might think years of struggling is bad, but in God's terms, it is not that long.

With that, keep in mind that our negative feelings and emotions attached to the struggle we are facing will gradually transform into new meaning over *time*. Have you ever heard of the idiom "Time heals all wounds"? Well, if you have not, now you have. Merriam-Webster describes it as the "notion of sadness, disappointment, etc., gradually goes away as time passes." You might have also heard of a similar phrase when friends may have told you that "Time will tell" whether you and your significant other will remain friends or not after a sudden breakup. You might have even be reminded of this while listening to the lyrics of Colbie Caillat's hit song, "Realize," "It takes time to realize this all could pass you by."

In all essence, in order to persevere, you need to trust in timing and keep faith in the roadmap designed for your individual and unique life. In time, the right people will come into your life when you least expect it to help you find grace with your circumstances. If you become impatient, reflect on the blessings in your life now, engage in activities you enjoy, and spend time with people who inspire you. Take a deep breath and watch your life unfold before your eyes. This sense of peace will help you stand firm and hold on.

Reflect

What do you feel pressured with by time, and how can you efficiently utilize it?

Chapter 17

Creating Memories

*Memory is a way of holding on to the things you love, the
things you are, the things you never want to lose.*

—KEVIN ARNOLD

Before you begin to read this chapter, I want to inform
you that it may sound a little somber at first. I encourage
you to read through because it is the message behind the
emotions that will inspire you to change the way you
approach similar experiences. Whenever we are going
through a tough time, I have found that creating subtle
uplifting memories can be the main tools that help us
get through our storms and help us persevere.

This was the case for me and my family in 2016. We
were unprepared for a series of unpredictable and sudden events, and this was one of them: Cousin Tony was
diagnosed with glioblastoma multiforme stage IV brain
cancer, a terminal illness with no cure.

This was a lot for us to handle, but what got us through the pain were the memories we cherished and made. The story that I want to focus on here is of Tony. The sixteen months he had left to live were full of chemotherapy, radiation, and three different brain surgeries, but before his death, his daughter Stephanie created everlasting memories from love which helped her persevere through her loss.

For anyone reading this who is dealing with a loss, remember this quote from Brian Weiss, M.D., *Only Love is Real:*

Death is not an accident... we are given the opportunity to learn important lessons. They are teachers to us, teaching us about the values, priorities, and most of all about love. Often the most important lessons arise from the most difficult times.

Story Time
The twenty-four years that I had my dad in my life were so full, loving, and supportive because of the memories we attempted to make when he was alive. Even though he is gone today, I can be anywhere and feel his presence. I have only been to this cemetery three times, the two times I came back to New York from Europe, where I work, I did not even go to

the cemetery. I do not need to go there to feel him. I feel his love everywhere, and it is because of the memories we made.

My father's business demeanor had a major influence on me. He was in real estate. He started very small and then grew larger and larger. He bought houses, fixed them with his bare hands, and sold or rented them. He came from a blue collar background. When my mom moved to America, they were living in a basement with no windows. They just slowly started growing this business. I remember my dad even saying that when I was born in the hospital, he couldn't even afford to pay for when I was born.

Because my father was a self-made businessman, I always had business-focused conversations with him. I would come up with these contracts and negotiations with my dad for as long as I could remember. There was one that we made that said if I helped shave his back (thanks to our Italian-Greek blood) ten times, he would pay me. I got up to four shaves, and then lost the contract—ha! We would even play games like driving around streets and guessing how much each house sold for, or guess the square footage in the house.

When he was diagnosed with cancer, I started to circle back to these memories and wanted to continue to make more. I remember saying to myself, 'Okay, I have a little over a year to truly say goodbye to him and make the best of it.'

One day, I was going to visit him in the hospital after business hours. The lights were going to be all turned off, and it was going to be still and silent. I thought this would have been the best time to do something spontaneous and lighthearted and memorable.

His taste was a bit gone from chemotherapy, but I wanted to make the most of our situation. My father loved pepperoni pizza, like a classic Italian-American. I stopped at a place to buy him a slice and snuck in a mini-version of his favorite bottle of red wine and two plastic cups.

When I got to the room, I said 'Daddy, look what I snuck in,' and pulled out the bottle of wine. We smiled. It was fun, playful, light, and humor-filled. His eyes lit up like a child and looked at me with that endearing 'You're always going to be my little girl' expression.

We had a beautiful hour together. In that moment, I felt like he came back. It was us again like the old days. It was so fulfilling and beautiful. And this was just one memory that I hold tight.

Action Plan and Lesson

This was a short chapter, but the message behind it is important—slow down and enjoy the small moments.

Memories you hold on to can get you through tough times. Although it might be easier to get caught up in remembering every painstaking moment, it is important to keep track of the good ones as well.

Life is not what One lived, but what One remembers and how One remembers it in order to recount it.

—Gabriel Garcia Marquez

So, if we try to remember the good during the bad, we can change the whole meaning of our outcome. These memories can fuel us and make us persevere in the long run. As time passes, the little recollections you make can become the tools to help keep your head aboveground and stay resilient.

Just like Stephanie, I experienced similar memories when I was in the wake of my storm. It was always the small things that lit me up. Some of my greatest memories were the simple and effortless ones, like receiving text messages from unexpected acquaintances or cards in the mail from family members. I want to share some of my favorite ones with you.

Similar to Tony and Stephanie, my brother was the light in some of my worst days. "Hey Lex, I brought you some bread," Paul would say as he surprised me in my room with a piece of slightly toasted plain slice of Italian bread, just the way I like it, to make me feel less nauseous as I was hunched over in pain.

My mother and I shared a food-inspired memory of our own, which became a tradition. After each treatment, we walked to Dough Doughnuts at Urbanspace by Grand Central Terminal and tried a different flavor each time. It did not matter how sick I felt, this was the one thing that kept my spirits high.

There were other memories I have that had to do with receiving the grace of strangers. Like the times when I came home to get-well packages from people I did not even know. Or the time someone unexpectedly snuck an envelope on the table in a restaurant while I was crying in my mother's arms. I opened it, and it was a 3D pop-out card of flowers with the message: "Some flowers for you to cheer you up! Take care, from Holland."

One day, I came home after treatment to a large, heavy box sitting outside my door. It was a surprise to me. My curiosity grew because of the ambiguity behind it all. I did not order anything, and the return address was mysterious. I slowly pushed the box into my front entrance, ran to my desk to grab a pair of scissors, and began to open the cardboard flaps. Books! There was a detox cookbook, a coloring book, *Wreck this Journal* by Keri Smith, *Kitchen Table Wisdom: Stories that Heal* by Rachel Naomi Remen, *Everyday Grace: Having Hope, Finding Forgiveness, and Making Miracles* by Marianne Williamson, *The Book of Joy: Lasting Happiness in a Changing World* by Dalai Lama and Desmond Tutu, which are now some of my all-time favorites, to name a few. At the bottom of the box was a card from four of my friends from college.

These little moments I talked about became my tokens of hope. I now use these stories to fuel my life and try to go out of my way to make others experience similar blessings. With that being said, I encourage you to show your love to someone, to do something memorable for a loved one going through their battle, or even create a memory for yourself. Be spontaneous, do something bold, and learn to live because it will create a memory from an act of love and kindness. They are priceless.

Sometimes you will never know the value of a moment until it becomes a memory.

—Dr. Seuss

Reflect

What type of memory are you willing to create?

Chapter 18

Scripting Your New Life

Infuse your life with action. Don't wait for it to happen. Make it happen. Make your own future. Make your own hope. Make your own love. And whatever your beliefs, honor your creator, not by passively waiting for grace to come down from upon high, but by doing what you can to make grace happen...yourself, right now, right down here on Earth.

—BRADLEY WHITFORD

What I have learned from going through my traumatic experience of cancer is that after hitting rock bottom, there really is nowhere else to go but up. This is the lowest point any of us can visit. The only way out is up. This is your time to "Reach for the sky," as Woody from *Toy Story* puts it.

Sometimes it is difficult to change your mindset. I battled with pessimism from time to time and had moments of doubt, that cancer would come back. I knew that I would be free from my emotional pain if I stayed consistent by creating positive affirmations, like I discussed previously, but more specifically if I scripted the life I wanted to live in the future.

Purchasing a notebook and practicing this form of writing prospective feelings in present tense onto paper encouraged me to believe that a cancer-free life was possible. It continued to keep my faith high. Sure enough, it worked. To this day, anytime something dreadful happens to me, I turn to my pen and notepad and start to jot down feelings I want to experience in the future.

The reason I hand wrote phrases was because it had the most effectiveness. A study done by Indiana University stated that writing by hand "increases neural activity in certain sections of the brain, much like meditation." We read how meditation had scientific success, so why not try this practice as well? You can reinvent your story with the simple activity of scripting. I wrote down all the positive moments I wished to experience, worked toward them, and then experienced the outcomes.

Here are some of the few phrases I wrote down:

- I am fueling myself with foods that are helping heal and regenerate my body and am grateful for how much they are energizing me and allowing me to prosper.
- I am proud of myself for living my life through strength.
- I feel humbled by the way I am helping heal others and am successfully living my dreams and changing the world.

Dr. Amelia Aldao, licensed clinical psychologist and health care consultant, specifically explains how writing can be a successful tool for getting in touch with emotions and reducing their intensity.

The first time that we learn about something bad, we might be like, 'Oh my gosh, what is going on?' And then we can take a second, and realize that it is not as bad [as we initially thought]. Writing allows you get a different perspective of both the good and bad. It can help with the difficult moments. It allows you to see [on paper] the things that are hard to face.

When you're feeling really emotional about a topic, it is hard to become rational. That is why a therapist or counselor becomes important. [They can help you] practice mindfulness.

In intense moments, you can take a step back and develop awareness of what's going on around you, how you're feeling, and then take note of it. This can help gain perspective.

Story Time

Emilee Garfield, known as @cancersavedmylife on Instagram, experienced a similar mind shift as I did through the art of authoring her own life. Emilee has been through a series of trauma her whole life. She was born with a rare connective-tissue cancer called embryonal rhabdomyosarcoma after doctors discovered a tumor the size of a softball by her bladder and pelvis at the age of four. She underwent two years of chemotherapy and radiation. In the middle of it all, when she five, her father committed suicide.

Throughout her life, she was deeply affected by these two agonies. Cancer specifically made her develop shame. She thought of it as a curse.

I hated myself and my body. I shamed my body and was embarrassed of my scars. I became known as 'the girl that had cancer.' I wanted to be the cute girl in the bikini, but I did not value myself. I searched for affection and attention, and craved men to validate my worth and fill my void from the loss of my father. I found myself in toxic relationships and was trying to fulfill happiness by pleasing other people at my own expense. I wasn't living for me, but for others.

What happened next was the biggest wakeup call of my life. At the age of thirty-nine, I was diagnosed with stage 3C ovarian cancer. It was scary because it had a high recurrence rate and a low survival rate. I endured twenty weeks of chemotherapy and had two major surgeries, one leaving me with an ileostomy, aka a colostomy, bag attached to my side.

When I was diagnosed with cancer for the second time, I said to myself, 'I am going to change to be the person that I have always wanted to be.' I needed to find myself and start doing things for me. I had to shift my mindset.

Emilee paved her way through transformation by taking a life coaching course called *New Life Story Coaching* with Dr. David Krueger. This focused on how to change perspective on a life story through neuroscience and psychology. After taking the program, Emilee learned how to set boundaries and take care of and love herself. She realized that every single person has a story that weighs them down, but it is what we do with it that makes the difference.

Following this process, she began to apply the *Live A New Life Story* ROADMAP in her life. She used this seven-step roadmap to catapult her life:

Recognize Authorship of Your Life Story
Own Your Story
Assess the Storylines and Plot
Decide What You Want to Change
Map Changes
Author New Experiences
Program New Identity to Incorporate and Sustain the Changes

The way Emilee was able to personally do this was by focusing on creating peace and eliminating chaos. She removed all toxic people from her life and changed the relationship she had with herself. Emilee started to send herself love and compassion. She told herself that she was worthy of everything and anything.

This inspired her to script. She wrote notes and journal entries to herself every single day with positive healing phrases like "I forgive you" and "I love you." She even started to write down things she always wanted to do, like become an author of a book, make a new website, and start a nonprofit, all of which she ended up doing after completing the last phase of the ROADMAP.

Before she was able to fulfill her dreams, she had to create a new identity. Instead of labeling herself with the word "cancer," she recognized that her illness was just a piece of her overall story. It was going to give her the opportunity to be a healer for others.

Afterward, she finally had the courage to write *Reclaim Your Strength and Hope: Exercises For Cancer Core Recovery*, start emileegarfield.com, and register Cancer Core Recovery Project as an official 501(c)(3), which provides instructional online training to women with pelvic and abdominal cancers. Through this, she helps women who have undergone TRAM Flap reconstruction surgeries to help restore their body, just like she did with her own experience.

My motto became, 'progress, not perfection.' It was through this program that I realized that we are the only ones who can fix ourselves. It takes work, but everyone needs to invest in themselves because they deserve it.

There was a period before I was diagnosed with ovarian cancer when I was very lonely. I was depressed. I hit rock bottom. I ended up in a psych ward and wanted to die. It wasn't until the psychologists listened to my story and said, 'I understand.'

At that moment, I realized I wasn't alone. Someone else was able to relate to my pain, and there were even more people out there struggling like me. This helped me develop my passion to help women love themselves and see their worth, especially after cancer. I was able to figure out how, and now I am helping others.

Remember that once you hit rock bottom, there is one way to go, and it is up. You will see the light because you are the light. Everything you will ever need is right there, inside of you. Try not to worry; rather, surrender to your emotions and trust that the universe has your back.

I encourage you to dream big. 'Go Big or Go Home' are the words my oncologist told me the day I was diagnosed. I live by these words, and I want to pass them to others who need hope and inspiration—they really work! If I was able to fulfill all of these things, so can you.

Action Plan and Lesson

If you have not realized from not only reading this last chapter, but throughout the whole book, you are ultimately the author of your story and create your own outcome. Even in times of feeling hopeless, visualizing your life through scripting can give you the opportunity to undergo restorative physical and mental transformation. If you have exciting thoughts of freeing yourself of pain, then it will happen: all you need to do is believe in it to help you persevere in the long-run.

If creating a new life for yourself feels stressful, face those emotions, just like Dr. Aldalo said. They will make you stressed in the short run, but in the long run, they will allow you to grow and gain a different perspective just like Emilee. Her life turned around completely just because she started to engage in the activity of scripting the story she wanted to tell.

The power of writing is something I strongly believe in, as advocated by Emilee. Whenever I speak to a licensed professional about my feelings, I always make sure to bring my journal to reflect on my week's thoughts and then take note on ways to make improvements.

Reflect
What is the new life story you want to tell yourself?

Chapter 19

Moving Forward

Nothing lasts forever—pain and troubles included.

—*PAULO COELHO*

Before this book comes to an end, I have one more suggestion for you—fearlessly take action to move forward. I know from the bottom of my heart that you have the capability to work through your challenges. I have lived through it all, and on the other side, as a cancer survivor, I can assure you that there is so much hope, light, and beauty in this world that you can experience, even past your pain.

I still have my days of sorrow, but my gracious spirit has allowed for me to remember the better days ahead. I have become an optimist, and the many action plans mentioned in the previous chapters have given me peace with myself and my purpose. There were moments of doubt when I did not think I could get strong again, but I did. My worst nightmare was the best thing that happened to me because it allowed me to see that there is a way out of pain.

If I endured the most burdensome season of my life, cancer, you can get through yours as well. And if you do not think you can get past your present struggle, circle back to Chapter 10. Use the words that Jesus told me, "Do not worry, everything is going to be okay," to encourage you to push through. I believe he shared these words not only for my sake, but to comfort you. He knows that at the end of the day, there is more to your life here on Earth.

All you have to do is use the inner strength within your soul to become resilient. You were made to prosper, and your challenges are here to help you grow. Accept your reality, live in the present moment, fight your fears, believe in the unimaginable, use your intuition, have faith in a larger energy force, be patient with your time, and use available resources around you. Connect with others and start conversations. You are not alone, and your story can save someone else, as theirs can help transform you into the best human being you were set to be. Use these stories that you have read about as tickets to transformation.

Lastly, do not rush the process, but trust in it. Trust the battle. Trust the struggle. Trust yourself. Trust *it*, and know you have the power to persevere.

Chapter 20

Author Your
Own Story

Reflecting back on the last chapter, I want you to use the space in this section as a place to take notes on your thoughts and feelings, script your new journey, and believe in the magic of it all.

_____

_____

_____

_____

_____

_____

_____

_____

_____

_____

You should never view your challenges as a disadvantage. Instead, it's important for you to understand that your experience facing and overcoming adversity is actually one of your biggest advantages.

—Michelle Obama

_____

_____

_____

_____

_____

_____

*Consult not your fears but your
hopes and your dreams. Think
not about your frustrations, but
about your unfulfilled potential.
Concern yourself not with what you
tried and failed in, but with what
it is still possible for you to do.*

—Pope John XXIII

_____

_____

_____

_____

_____

_____

_____

_____

_____

_____

_____

_____

*Imagination is the beginning of
creation. You imagine what you
desire, you will what you imagine,
and at last you create what you will.*

—George Bernard Shaw

_____

_____

_____

_____

_____

_____

_____

_____

_____

Works Referenced

Introduction

Baker, Paul. "Tony Robbins – Hour of Power." Just in (down) Time, April 13, 2015. https://justindowntime.wordpress.com/2014/12/28/tony-robbins-hour-of-power/.

Byrne, Rhonda. *The Magic:* New York, NY: Atria Books, 2012.

"Hodgkin's Lymphoma." MD Anderson Cancer Center. Accessed February 11, 2019. https://www.mdanderson.org/cancer-types/hodgkins-lymphoma.html.

Sreenivasan, N. S., and V. Narayana. *Continual Improvement Process*. Delhi, India: Pearson Power, 2008.

Chapter I

O'Donohue, John. *Anam cara: a Book of Celtic Wisdom*. New York: Harper Perennial, 2004.

Osteen, Joel. YouTube. YouTube, August 21, 2016. https://www.
youtube.com/watch?v=D5S0C35f_gE.

Ray, Amit. *Meditation: Insights and Inspirations*. Second Edi-
tioned. Inner Light Publishers, n.d.

Chapter 2

Carmen, Allison. "Acceptance." *10 Minutes to Less Suffering*.
Podcast audio, December 7, 2017. http://tenminutestoless-
suffering.libsyn.com/acceptance

King, Jawara D. *Transform Your World Through the Powers of
Your Mind: A Guide to Planetary Transformation and Spiritual
Enlightenment*. Bloomington, IN: AuthorHouse , 2009.

Chapter 3

Dispenza, Joe. *You Are the Placebo: Making Your Mind Matter*.
Carlsbad, CA: Hay House, Inc., 2015.

Ronaldson, Amy, Gerard J Molloy, Anna Wikman, Lydia Poole,
Juan-Carlos Kaski, and Andrew Steptoe. "Optimism and
Recovery after Acute Coronary Syndrome: a Clinical
Cohort Study." Psychosomatic medicine. Lippincott Wil-
liams & Wilkins, April 2015. https://www.ncbi.nlm.nih.
gov/pmc/articles/PMC4396437/.

"The Average Person Has between 12,000 and 60,000 Thoughts per Day." Siobhan Kelleher Kukolic, June 11, 2018. https://siobhankukolic.com/the-average-person-has-between-12000-and-60000-thoughts-per-day/.

Wayne Dyer - When You Change the Way You Look at Things. YouTube. YouTube, 2008. https://www.youtube.com/watch?v=urQPraeeYow.

Chapter 4

Generational Wealth Family. "Bishop TD Jakes: Fear Is Holding You Back!!!." YouTube. Oct 30, 2015. https://www.youtube.com/watch?v=8nkYIEkqLgc

Mehr-Muska, Tracy W. *Weathering the Storm: Simple Strategies for Being Peaceful and Prepared.* Eugene, OR: Resource Publications, 2019.

Research. "Did You Know... The Facts About Young Adults and Cancer?" OncoLink. Accessed April 14, 2019. https://www.oncolink.org/support/resources/resources-for-young-adults/did-you-know-the-facts-about-young-adults-and-cancer.

Chapter 5

Menninger, M.D. William C. "Psychological Aspects Of Hobbies." *American Journal of Psychiatry* 99, no. 1 (1942): 122–29. https://doi.org/10.1176/ajp.99.1.122.

Nawalkha, Ajit. *Live Big: the Entrepreneurs Guide to Passion, Practicality, and Purpose.* Dallas, TX: BenBella Books, Inc., 2018.

Chapter 6

Pfaff, Chris "Drama." "#144 - Jay Shetty | Living As a Monk for 3 Years." *Short Story Long.* Podcast Audio, March 20, 2019 https://podbay.fm/podcast/1111787417/e/1553065200

Teri Garr Quotes. BrainyQuote.com, BrainyMedia Inc, 2019. https://www.brainyquote.com/quotes/teri_garr_289556, accessed June 19, 2019.

Chapter 7

Crumpler, David. "Two Actresses with Jacksonville Ties Star in New Oprah Winfrey Network Show." The Florida Times-Union. The Florida Times-Union, May 28, 2013. https://www.jacksonville.com/entertainment/2013-05-28/story/two-actresses-jacksonville-ties-star-new-oprah-winfrey-network-show.

Phipps, Wintley, and James L. Lund. *Your Best Destiny: Becoming the Person You Were Created to Be.* Carol Stream, IL: Tyndale Momentum, an Imprint of Tyndale House Publishers, Inc., 2015.

Chapter 8

A Course in Miracles. Glen Elen, CA: Foundation for Inner Peace, 1992.

"An Attitude of Gratitude." The Chopra Center, March 31, 2017. https://chopra.com/free-programs/attitude-of-gratitude.

"Belief." Merriam-Webster. Merriam-Webster. Accessed June 16, 2019. https://www.merriam-webster.com/dictionary/belief.

FOY, TERRI SAVELLE. *DREAM IT - PIN IT - LIVE IT: Make Vision Boards Work for You.* S.l.: TERRI SAVELLE FOY MINISTE, 2015.

Ronaldson, Amy, Gerard J Molloy, Anna Wikman, Lydia Poole, Juan-Carlos Kaski, and Andrew Steptoe. "Optimism and Recovery after Acute Coronary Syndrome: a Clinical Cohort Study." Psychosomatic medicine. Lippincott Williams & Wilkins, April 2015. https://www.ncbi.nlm.nih.gov/pmc/articles/PMC4396437/.

Chapter 9

Aeschylus, E. H., and E. H. Plumptre. *The Tragedies of Aeschylos: a New Translation*. Philadelphia: David McKay, 1899.

Holy Bible New International Version, Witness Edition. Holy Bible New International Version, Witness Edition. Zondervan, 2015.

Price, Steven D. *The Quotable Billionaire: Advice and Reflections From and For the Real, Former, Almost, and Wanna-Be Super-Rich . . . and Others*. New York, NY: Skyhorse Pub., 2009.

Chapter 10

Holy Bible New International Version, Witness Edition. Holy Bible New International Version, Witness Edition. Zondervan, 2015.

Illsley, C.L. "Largest Religions In The World." WorldAtlas, March 21, 2016. https://www.worldatlas.com/articles/largest-religions-in-the-world.html.

"It's Time to Remember Love." It's time to remember Love. Accessed August 11, 2019. https://www.lovescurriculum.com/.

Joyce Meyer Quotes. BrainyQuote.com, BrainyMedia Inc, 2019. https://www.brainyquote.com/quotes/joyce_meyer_565139, accessed October 8, 2019.

Richardson, Alan, and John Bowden. *The Westminster Dictionary of Christian Theology*. Philadelphia: Westminster Press, 2005.

Chapter 11

Choquette, Sonia. *The Time Has Come…: To Accept Your Intuitive Gifts!* Carlsbad, CA: Hay House, Inc., 2008.

Endometriosis.org. "Facts about Endometriosis „ Endometriosis.org." Endometriosis.org. Accessed September 9, 2019. http://endometriosis.org/resources/articles/facts-about-endometriosis/.

Eternal-Thoughts Law of Attraction. "Abraham Hicks 2017–Always do what your intuition says(new)." YouTube. Apr 12, 2017. https://www.youtube.com/watch?v=y7CWmFRr3Co.

"Jay Pasricha, M.B.B.S., M.D., Professor of Medicine." Johns Hopkins Medicine. Accessed August 14, 2019. https://www.hopkinsmedicine.org/profiles/results/directory/profile/8897935/pankaj-pasricha.

Maxwell, John C. *No Limits. Blow the CAP Off Your Capacity* New York: Center Street, 2018.

"Spiritual Awareness Circle & Our Community of Love & Light." Meetup. Accessed October 13, 2019. https://www. meetup.com/SAC-OCLL/pages/17730152/Who_or_What_ is_Abraham-Hicks/.

Stuckey, Heather L, and Jeremy Nobel. "The Connection between Art, Healing, and Public Health: a Review of Current Literature." American journal of public health. American Public Health Association, February 2010. https:// www.ncbi.nlm.nih.gov/pmc/articles/PMC2804629/.

"3 Reasons Why You Are Seeing 777 – The Meaning of 777." Willow Soul. Accessed March 17, 2018. https://willowsoul. com/blogs/numbers/3-reasons-why-you-are-seeing-777- the-meaning-of-777.

"Spiritual Awareness Circle & Our Community of Love & Light." Meetup. Accessed October 13, 2019. https://www. meetup.com/SAC-OCLL/pages/17730152/Who_or_What_ is_Abraham-Hicks/.

Chapter 12

Chappus, Jesse, and Marni Wasserman. "089: Dr. Josh Axe – Eat Dirt · Leaky Gut Is The Root Cause Of All Disease · Soil-Based Organisms." The Ultimate Health Podcast Audio, March 28, 2016. https://www.stitcher.com/podcast/

the-ultimate-health-podcast/e/089-dr-josh-axe-eat-dirt-leaky-gut-is-the-root-cause-43578477

Dean, Jeremy. *Making Habits, Breaking Habits: Why We Do Things, Why We Don't, and How to Make Any Change Stick.* Richmond: Oneworld, 2013.

Gabriel, Roger, Roger Gabriel, and Chopra Center Educator. "8 Types of Meditation Explained." The Chopra Center, March 7, 2019. https://chopra.com/articles/8-types-of-meditation-explained.

Hensel, John E. *YOU, Inc.: The Most Important Enterprise in the Twenty-First Century.* New York: iUniverse, 2004.

Hoge, Elizabeth A, Eric Bui, Luana Marques, Christina A Metcalf, Laura K Morris, Donald J Robinaugh, John J Worthington, Mark H Pollack, and Naomi M Simon. "Randomized Controlled Trial of Mindfulness Meditation for Generalized Anxiety Disorder: Effects on Anxiety and Stress Reactivity." The Journal of clinical psychiatry. U.S. National Library of Medicine, August 2013. https://www.ncbi.nlm.nih.gov/pubmed/23541163.

"Judgment Detox. Release the Beliefs That Hold You Back from Living A Better Life." Goodreads. Goodreads,

January 2, 2018. https://www.goodreads.com/book/show/35297340-judgment-detox.

"Limbic System: Amygdala (Section 4, Chapter 6) Neuroscience Online: An Electronic Textbook for the Neurosciences: Department of Neurobiology and Anatomy - The University of Texas Medical School at Houston." Limbic System: Amygdala (Section 4, Chapter 6) Neuroscience Online: An Electronic Textbook for the Neurosciences | Department of Neurobiology and Anatomy - The University of Texas Medical School at Houston. Accessed September 1, 2019. https://nba.uth.tmc.edu/neuroscience/m/s4/chapter06.html.

"Loving-Kindness Meditation (Greater Good in Action)." Greater Good in Action - Science-based Practices for a Meaningful Life. Accessed June 25, 2019. https://ggia.berkeley.edu/practice/loving_kindness_meditation#data-tab-why_you_should_try_it.

"Massachusetts General Hospital." Massachusetts General Hospital, Boston, Massachusetts - Massachusetts General Hospital, Boston, MA. Accessed September 1, 2019. https://www.massgeneral.org/research/researchlab.aspx?id=1153.

"MGH Chelsea HealthCare Center Community Research Day."
MGH Chelsea HealthCare Center Community Research Day.
Chelsea, MA: MGH Chelsea HealthCare Center, 2018.

"Mindfulness Changes Brain Structure in Eight Weeks."
Action for Happiness. Accessed September 1, 2019. https://
www.actionforhappiness.org/news/mindfulness-changes-
brain-structure-in-eight-weeks.

Mindworks Team Mindworks. "What Are the Different Types
of Meditation? Benefits (With Examples)." Mindworks
Meditation, August 29, 2019. https://mindworks.org/blog/
different-types-meditation-technique/.

Ray, Amit. *Meditation: Insights and Inspirations.* Second Edi-
tioned. Inner Light Publishers, n.d.

"What Are the Solfeggio Frequencies?" Attuned Vibrations.
Accessed October 9, 2019. https://attunedvibrations.com/
solfeggio/.

"What Is Meditation?" Headspace. Accessed October 1, 2019.
https://www.headspace.com/meditation-101/what-is-med-
itation.

Chapter 13

Coppola, Gloria Kuuleialoha. *Both Ends of the Rainbow: Lomi-lomi ~ a Healing Journey*. Bloomington, IN: Balboa Press, 2013.

Duval, Jared. *Next Generation Democracy: What the Open-Source Revolution Means for Power ...* New York, NY: Bloomsbury USA, 2010.

Stuckey, Heather L, and Jeremy Nobel. "The Connection between Art, Healing, and Public Health: a Review of Current Literature." American journal of public health. American Public Health Association, February 2010. https://www.ncbi.nlm.nih.gov/pmc/articles/PMC2804629/#bib68.

Words of Art: Inspiring Quotes from the Masters. Avon, MA: Adams Media, 2013.

Chapter 14

Kaskel, Dr. Michael, and R.N. Larry Kaskel. *Dr. Kaskel's Living In Wellness, Volume One: Let Food Be Thy Medicine*. Place of publication not identified: LULU Publishing SERVICES, 2014.

Loyola Press. "Guardian Angel Prayer." Guardian Angel
Prayer. Loyola Press, April 20, 2016. https://www.loyol-
apress.com/our-catholic-faith/prayer/traditional-cath-
olic-prayers/prayers-every-catholic-should-know/
guardian-angel-prayer.

"Mary Anne Radmacher Quotes (Author of Lean Forward
Into Your Life)." Goodreads. Goodreads. Accessed July 9,
2019. https://www.goodreads.com/author/quotes/149829.
Mary_Anne_Radmacher.

Chapter 15

"Abraham Maslow." The Pursuit of Happiness. Pursuit of Happiness, Inc.. Accessed 9AD. https://www.pursuit-of-happi-
ness.org/history-of-happiness/abraham-maslow/.

Charles Kennedy Quotes. BrainyQuote.com, BrainyMedia Inc,
2019. https://www.brainyquote.com/quotes/charles_ken-
nedy_720234, accessed October 03, 2019.

Hyman, Mark. "8 Ways to Take Charge of Your Health." Dr.
Mark Hyman, February 26, 2019. https://drhyman.com/
blog/2019/02/26/8-ways-to-take-charge-of-your-health/.

Manns, Mary Lynn., and Linda Rising. *More Fearless Change: Strategies for Making Your Ideas Happen.* Upper Saddle River, NJ: Addison-Wesley, 2015.

Chapter 16

Caillat, Colbie. "Realize." *Coco.*, Universal Republic Records, 2007. *Amazon*, https://www.amazon.com/Realize/dp/B000VAMKRA

"Time Heals All Wounds." Merriam-Webster. Merriam-Webster. Accessed August 9, 2019. https://www.merriam-webster.com/dictionary/time heals all wounds.

"Rebekah Letch." Rebekah Letch - The universe is not trying to break you,... Accessed September 25, 2019. https://www.facebook.com/rebekahletch/photos/the-universe-is-not-trying-to-break-you-my-dear-its-trying-to-find-a-way-to-wake/688901327966651/.

Chapter 17

Barnum, Melanie. *Psychic Vision: Developing Your Clairvoyant and Remote Viewing Skills.* Woodbury, MN: Llewellyn Publications, 2015.

Jones. *Survive and Thrive Against the Odds.* Xlibris, LLC., 2014.

Tiberghien, Susan M. *One Year to a Writing Life: Twelve Lessons to Deepen Every Writer's Art and Craft*. New York: Marlowe & Co., 2007.

Weiss, Brian. *Only Love Is Real: The Story of Soulmates Reunited*. London: Piatkus, 2000.

Chapter 18

Bounds, Gwendolyn. The Wall Street Journal. Dow Jones & Company, October 5, 2010. https://www.wsj.com/articles/ SB10001424052748704631504575531932754922518#articleTabs=article.

Jones, Jasmine. *Toy Story 3 Junior Novel*. Pixar, 2010.

"New Life Story® Wellness Coaches Training." MentorPath. Accessed September 9, 2019. https://www.mentorpath. com/new-life-story-wellness-coaches-training/.

White, III Dr Samuel. *Hope for Your Soul: Words of Encouragement*. Place of publication not identified: WESTBOW Press, 2018.

Chapter 19

Coelho, Paulo. "Nothing Lasts Forever - Pain and Troubles Included." Twitter. Twitter, September 9, 2010. https://twitter.com/paulocoelho/status/24049544123.

Chapter 20

Harteveld, Casper. *Triadic Game Design: Balancing Reality, Meaning and Play.* London: Springer, 2011.

Mathuur, Viveck. *Cracking into Super Brains with 6000 Supreme Quotes.* New Delhi: Studera Press, 2017.

Ricci, Mary Cay. *Nothing You Can't Do!: The Secret Power of Growth Mindsets.* Waco, TX: Prufrock Press Inc., 2018.